T0170817

We Are Penn State

*The Remarkable Journey
of the 2012 Nittany Lions*

Lou Prato

TRIUMPH
B O O K S

Library of Congress Cataloging-in-Publication Data

Prato, Lou.
  We are Penn State : the remarkable journey of the 2012 Nittany Lions / Lou Prato.
    pages cm
  ISBN 978-1-60078-862-8 (hardback)
1. Pennsylvania State University—Football. 2. Penn State Nittany Lions (Football team) I. Title.
  GV958.P46P74 2013
  796.332'630974853—dc23

                        2013023561

This book is available in quantity at special discounts for your group or organization. For further information, contact:
  Triumph Books LLC
  814 North Franklin Street
  Chicago, Illinois 60610
  (312) 337-0747
  www.triumphbooks.com

Printed in U.S.A.

ISBN: 978-1-60078-862-8

Design by Patricia Frey

To all the coaches, players, and staff of the 2012 Penn State football team; to their families who supported them through one of the most unique years any team has ever endured in the history of college football; and to the nearly 1,000 Penn State football lettermen and all the Nittany Lions fans who stood solidly behind them all the way. We Are…Penn State!

"Every man has his own destiny: the only imperative is to follow it, to accept it, no matter where it leads him."

—Henry Miller

Contents

Foreword *by Bill O'Brien*   **ix**

Introduction *2012 Season*   **xiii**

Prologue *The Turmoil Begins*   **xvii**

Chapter 1 *The Search*   **1**

Chapter 2 *The Torch Is Passed*   **11**

Chapter 3 *There's a New Sheriff in Town*   **25**

Chapter 4 *It Happens Every Spring*   **35**

Chapter 5 *The Long, Hot Summer*   **47**

Chapter 6 *Hell Week Plus One*   **65**

Chapter 7 *It's Us Against the World*   **81**

Chapter 8 *"The Times They Are A-Changin'"*   **97**

Chapter 9 *A Kick In the Butt*   **117**

Chapter 10 *The Bleeding Stops*   **131**

Chapter 11 *Revenge Is Sweet*   **145**

Chapter 12 *Sometimes You Eat the Bear,*
Sometimes the Bear Eats You **167**

Chapter 13 *Completed Mission* **181**

Chapter 14 *Hail to the Lions* **205**

Acknowledgments **219**

Appendix I *Penn State's 2012 Senior Class* **221**

Appendix II *Links to Internet Videos* **225**

Foreword

The 2012 football season was one of the most gratifying in my 20 years of coaching college and professional football. I could not be more proud of the young men who played for me. They are what Penn State is all about. We went through a lot together, and they gave all they had on the field and off.

I can't say enough about these players, especially our seniors and their leadership. This was just a fantastic senior class. I'm not sure what would have happened without them stepping up and keeping the team united. We faced many challenges and obstacles along the way, but the seniors were always there to help their teammates and the coaches. You'll see all their names in this book. Whether they were starters or played mostly with our scout team—that scrappy group I call "the Dirty Show"—they were the heart and soul of our team and the epitome of our motto, "One Team."

It's not easy to single out any one or two of those seniors, but I have to mention our captains: Jordan Hill, Michael Mauti, Matt Stankiewitch, Michael Yancich, and Michael Zordich. During the season, I selected game captains each week, and that gave me the opportunity to publicly recognize the seniors for their leadership, dedication, work ethic, and loyalty. At the end of the season, the entire team voted and elected Jordan, Matt, and the three Michaels to be our captains. That tells you all you need to know about what these five young men meant to every one of us, including the loyal Penn State fans who stood by us all the way.

No college football team in history has had to go through what our players did in 2012. They had nothing to do with the events that led the NCAA to penalize Penn State with unprecedented sanctions. Those sanctions could have been disastrous to our team. However, rather than let the sanctions shatter team unity, we bonded together—the players, our coaches, and our entire football staff—and faced the challenges head-on.

We had a very difficult period when the NCAA announced those penalties in late July, but the worst time may have been after we lost our first two games. I know there were many people back then who thought the players were going to fold. That just made these kids practice harder to get better and better. They set their minds to do what they had to do to win—and they showed everyone the type of young men they are. They not only cared about football, but they also cared about getting an education and helping the community recover from the notoriety and embarrassment brought upon us by one individual. They had a chance to do something special, and they did it. And one of the things they did was demonstrate their strong support for the victims of child sex abuse by wearing blue ribbons on their uniforms at every game.

It all started way back in mid-February of 2012 with our first 5:30 AM workout in those freezing temperatures with Craig Fitzgerald, our strength-and-conditioning coach, and went right through to that great last play in overtime in the Wisconsin game at Beaver Stadium. You'll read all about those moments and many others in this book.

That's why this team deserves its place of honor in the ring at Beaver Stadium, alongside the greatest Penn State teams of the past. Now, 2012 is memorialized alongside the 1982 and 1986 national champions and the other undefeated and Big Ten championship teams that have made Penn State football one of the best programs in college football.

Because of my players, I received several awards as Coach of the Year, and none was better than the one named after one of the greatest coaches in football history: Paul "Bear" Bryant. I wish I could give every one of our players a piece of that trophy. They deserve the award as much as I do, and my assistant coaches do too.

No one was more pleased than me when the prestigious Maxwell Club honored our team with the Thomas Brookshier Spirit Award for "commitment, leadership, and outstanding effort." The players did it, led by a great group of seniors who showed all of us what loyalty means.

In 2012 our team showed everyone why "We Are…Penn State!"

—Bill O'Brien

Introduction

2012 Season

No one could have envisioned in the late summer of 2012 that the Penn State football team would be honored months later as one of the greatest teams in school history.

They didn't win a national championship or come close to one. Nor did they finish undefeated or win a Big Ten title. In fact, the team's final 8–4 record is modest at best.

Yet no team in college football ever had to face the problems and obstacles encountered by Penn State's 2012 team, starting with an off-field scandal of historic proportion that continues to reverberate beyond the world of college football.

What these proud Nittany Lions accomplished—particularly the senior class—and how they did it is the subject of this book. It was a remarkable journey and is told here in an unusual way—in the format of a diary.

This writer is part of the media and a Penn State sports historian. I have covered Penn State football sporadically since the mid-1950s and am the author of three books about Penn State football and the coauthor of two others. In 2000 I helped in the construction of the Penn State All-Sports Museum and was its first director from 2001 through 2005. I am also a fan, part of the vast

Nittany Nation that jams Beaver Stadium in the fall and follows the team on the road whenever possible.

Because of my background and my previous work with Triumph Books, the company believed I was the right person to write this diary.

Along the way, I used many stories from the media, particularly by Penn State football beat reporters, and the official files of Penn State's Athletic Communications Department, including transcripts of news conferences and postgame interviews. I also used video from various sources to write accurately about events that I did not attend in person.

What emerges is a diary that I think Penn State football fans can easily relate to. Each entry usually begins with my overall reflection on an event or a particular day, perhaps supplemented by additional information or information I could not have known at the time of the initial diary entry. This narrative text is then followed by my specific excerpts from my diary.

At one point, I intended to include the names of many of the most loyal fans whom I know—the ones I continue to see at the games, home and away. But alas, my space was limited, and even some of my initial diary notations had to be eliminated in the final editing.

Although I reflect upon each game of the 2012 season, this is a book about people—the players and coaches who achieved success on the field because of what they did off it.

Bill O'Brien is the catalyst who made it all happen. He may have been a rookie head coach, but he showed the intelligence, adaptability, and composure of a veteran. That not only won him the loyalty of the players he hardly knew but eventually the praise of his peers as Coach of the Year.

However, without those players who quickly grew to trust O'Brien and his assistants, this book would not have been written. Whether they were starters or walk-ons who rarely played or seniors or underclassmen making the best of their opportunities, they were all important to the success of the 2012 season.

Yet it was O'Brien himself who continually pointed to the senior leadership as the heart and soul of this team, and for that reason their names are listed in a brief appendix at the end of the book.

Three seniors in particular were at the center of the team's remarkable journey—legacy recruits Michael Mauti and Michael Zordich, born leaders who followed their fathers to become Nittany Lions forever, and Matt McGloin, the quarterback everyone seemed to doubt until a new head coach entrusted him with the fate of his new offense.

The 2012 season will be remembered forever in Penn State's proud football history. This diary is but a short chronicle of how it all transpired.

Prologue

The Turmoil Begins

Saturday, November 5, 2011

This is the day Penn State football changed forever.

It was an open date for the 2011 football team, after it had come from behind late in the fourth quarter in the snow and cold at Beaver Stadium one week earlier, on October 29, to beat Illinois 10–7 and move to 8–1 for the season, giving Coach Joe Paterno his record-setting 409th victory.

I could not believe I had to watch that historic October 29 game on television because of poor winter highway conditions between my home and the stadium 14 miles away.

With Penn State trailing 7–3 in a sloppily played game, backup junior quarterback Matt McGloin had led an 80-yard drive to set up a three-yard touchdown by Silas Redd with 1:08 left. Junior Anthony Fera's extra point made the score 10–7. By that time most of the announced crowd of 97,828 had left because of the wintry weather. Yet the fans who were still there had to sit through another tense minute in the eerie artificial lighting and freezing temperatures before watching an attempted Illinois field goal bounce off the right crossbar. That October 29 victory moved Paterno ahead of Grambling's

Eddie Robinson as the winningest coach in the NCAA, and I can still remember the TV sportscasts showing Penn State president Graham Spanier and athletics director Tim Curley happily congratulating Paterno in the crowded stadium media room after the game.

Little did any of us know October 29 would be the last game of Paterno's life. Nor were we aware that he, Spanier, and Curley would soon lose their jobs and suffer tarnished reputations—rightfully or wrongfully—in what the media now calls the biggest scandal in the history of college sports. At the time, we also would have found it ludicrous that the oft-maligned McGloin would be a key player in an unforgettable 2012 season, while Redd, Fera, and junior wide receiver Justin Brown—the three best offensive players on the 2011 team—would abandon their Nittany Lions teammates for personal reasons and transfer to other schools.

As the Lions faithful still basked in the glory of that October 29 victory, there was ugliness brewing. And on November 5, it broke. That Saturday morning, the Pennsylvania attorney general issued a press release announcing the arrest of retired assistant football coach Jerry Sandusky on 40 charges of sexual abuse of children, and the indictment of Tim Curley and Gary Schultz, the university's vice president for finance and business, on charges of perjury and failure to report Sandusky's alleged crimes.

The worldwide Penn State family was shocked by what we heard on radio and television and read on the Internet and in newspapers. No one could believe it. Sandusky, the football team's linebacker guru for nearly 30 years and defensive coordinator when he retired in 2000, was almost as revered as Paterno—not just for his football coaching but even more so because of the Second Mile charity he had created in 1977 to help underprivileged and wayward boys.

I began getting tips about the investigation of Sandusky from media friends in June 2009, and the rumors continued for almost two years before it became public knowledge in Sara Ganim's story about a grand jury investigation, published March 31, 2011, in the *(Harrisburg) Patriot-News* and *Centre Daily Times.* Ganim had been pursuing the rumors since the summer of 2009 while working for the *Centre Daily Times.*

Her second story about the investigation appeared on April 4, but Ganim's revelations were basically ignored by the rest of the media, except for a small item sent out by the Associated Press and a column in the *Beaver County Times*, and there was nothing more heard about it until the attorney general's news release today. Even though I'd heard considerably more about what Sandusky may have been up to, I was as shocked and revolted as anyone this morning as I read the attorney general's extensive 23-page report from the grand jury. I don't know Sandusky well but have interviewed him a few times and worked for several years as a volunteer at the Second Mile's popular golf tournament held every summer. This is very bad for Penn State and especially for the football team.

Tuesday, November 8, 2011

On Monday, November 7, Joe Paterno became the focal point of the Sandusky affair during an electrifying televised news conference in Harrisburg in which the attorney general outlined the charges resulting from the grand jury presentment. Toward the end of the news conference the commander of the Pennsylvania State Police, who was directly involved in the investigation while working for the previous attorney general (now the governor), told reporters that Paterno was morally responsible for Sandusky's alleged abuse of children for more than a decade. He offered no proof, but the media jumped at the inflammatory statement, and Paterno was condemned from coast to coast.

The next day, Tuesday, Paterno's regularly scheduled weekly news conference with reporters at Beaver Stadium was abruptly canceled about 30 minutes before its scheduled start, on orders of the Penn State Board of Trustees.

I was among the more than 250 local and national media waiting in line outside the Beaver Stadium tunnel to get into the media room today. Normally there are no more than a dozen or so local beat reporters and cameramen on hand for Paterno's weekly news conferences. This large group was unprecedented. When assistant athletics director Jeff Nelson read a brief statement announcing the cancellation, there was a sudden commotion, with reporters shouting questions at Nelson and asking each other what the hell was happening and why. The media was in a tizzy, and I didn't blame them. This awkward situation ignited by the trustees is only going to make everything worse unless the people in charge soon explain the reasons behind the cancellation. This makes it look terrible for Paterno and also for the university itself, which has a reputation among the media for stonewalling and a lack of openness.

Wednesday, November 9, 2011

The 46-year career of Joe Paterno as head football coach came to a stunning and sudden end when he was fired at about 8:00 PM in a short telephone call with the vice chair of the Penn State Board of Trustees. Earlier in the day, Paterno released a brief statement announcing his retirement at the end of the season, peripherally citing the scandal, the media, and public pressure on the trustees to dismiss him. At 8:45 the trustees notified defensive coordinator Tom Bradley, a former player who had spent 33 years as an assistant coach under Paterno, that he would be the interim head coach for the rest of the 2011 season. In a tense, hastily called news conference televised live at 10:00 PM, the trustees formally announced Paterno's dismissal, and it touched off an angry disturbance of some 2,500 to 4,000 students in downtown State College.

Video and photos of that "riot" are still vivid in the public's consciousness, and that long-lasting perception of a school and a football program that seems to care more about their legendary coach than the victims of child abuse is one the 2012 football team had to overcome from the moment it regrouped under a new head coach two months later.

Since the weekend, the national media has made Sandusky and Penn State the major story in the world, with 24-hour coverage on cable television, in newspapers, and on the Internet, causing a feeding frenzy that continues to escalate. As the hours and days pass, the media scrutiny and criticism only intensify, especially—and grossly and unfairly—on Paterno, with a torrent of angry demands for his firing almost from the day of Sandusky's arrest.

Paterno had previously clashed with several board members, and under this pressure his support weakened. His departure, one way or another, seemed inevitable. I am not surprised that it occurred, only by the late-night urgency and the inept and malevolent way it has been handled.

I believe the information should have been held until tomorrow, when the students were in class. State College police say they were given only about an hour's notice to prepare for what might happen when the announcement was made, and it should not surprise anyone—especially the trustees—that the students are having an emotional reaction.

The media instantly called the disturbance a riot, and technically, under the legal term, it is. However, it is being far overblown by the press and is giving the impression of an out-of-control university that is supporting, if not the child molester himself, an alleged cover-up and the involvement of Paterno. The students are wrong—and several have been jailed, with fines and possible expulsion sure to follow. What they really are doing is protesting the sudden dismissal of the head football coach they have come to love and respect after his more than 60 years of devotion to their university.

Thursday, November 10, 2011

In a televised news conference at 11:00 AM, at Beaver Stadium, Tom Bradley told a packed room that "a lot of [players] are in shock." He said he had telephoned the captains the previous night, and "a whole bunch of guys came over to the Lasch Building...and piled into my office and we discussed team matters." Then, following an early morning staff meeting, he said, there was a formal team meeting at 8:00 AM. He told reporters, "I grieve for the victims and the families. Our [team's] thoughts and our prayers are with them." But his main job was to get the team ready to play Nebraska on Saturday, and he said, "This team has put in a lot of hard work. Saturday will be Senior Day for many of them. They deserve to have this day." Several reporters asked about the players, and Bradley replied, "They have mixed emotions.... We have great leadership on this football team.... It is a very resilient group."

I was at the news conference, just as I had been at Paterno's weekly pregame news conferences in this same room since it was reconstructed in 2001. I almost always sat near the back of the room, in the first of three rows of theater seats and in front of where the local television stations set up their cameras. Fran Fisher, the retired and revered Penn State sportscaster, was my seat partner, and we usually kibitzed quietly during Paterno's exchanges with the media. We frequently joked about the three of us being the oldest guys in the room.

Fran and I marveled at the historic nature of what we were seeing today. For the first time in 46 years, there was a new head football coach responding to the reporters, and we were the only two in the room who were there at the beginning—in this stadium as part of the media covering Paterno's first game and his first season in 1966. There were only a handful of us back then, compared to the media horde of today. Newspapers were still king, with radio and television not far behind. Today it's a new world of 24-hour news, the Internet, and Twitter.

Times have changed, but college football is still a game played by 18-to-22-year-old young men, and their emotions and maturity are constantly changing as they face new challenges on and off the field. It's up to the more experienced and sophisticated coaches to help guide the younger players through all the tribulations and turbulence they encounter, serving virtually as second fathers. However, no football coach or player has ever been in such a unique and unfathomable situation of these Penn State coaches and players.

None of these players know Jerry Sandusky, and few have ever seen him. But primarily because of him, almost overnight, the Penn State football team has become the pariah of college football. I left the news conference thinking, *What happens from this point forward will not only affect each and every one of them personally but also the future reputation of my school, the Pennsylvania State University, and the lives of hundreds of thousands of Penn State alumni around the world.*

Saturday, November 12, 2011

Game Day: Nebraska at Beaver Stadium. Aside from the Sandusky arrest and Paterno firing, which had emotionally consumed the Penn State community, this was a vital football game. Nebraska had become a big rival since Penn State's controversial 1982 victory against the Huskers at Beaver Stadium, but this was the first game against Nebraska since it joined the Big Ten. The Huskers were 7–2, with both defeats in conference games. Despite Penn State's better ranking, the Huskers were a three-point favorite.

In looking back, there was something that happened that day that had a direct but subtle bearing on the surprising success of the 2012 team. On the Tuesday before the game, Rich Mauti, a player for Paterno in the mid-1970s who went on to play eight years in the NFL, sent some 800 emails to former lettermen encouraging them to be on the sideline for the Nebraska game to show support for Paterno and his team. Even after Paterno's firing, 317 were there.

Rich Mauti is at the soul of what Penn State football is all about. So are his two sons, Patrick and especially Michael—who became the heart of the unforgettable 2012 season. Rich was one of Paterno's few junior college transfers. He suffered a knee injury in 1973 that was so bad doctors said he would never play again. Another injury in the preseason of 1974 kept him off the field until the last three games of the season, but in 1975 and 1976 Rich was the team's best kick returner and a spot runner and receiver. Rich has lived in New Orleans since his playing days with the Saints, but Penn State is in his blood. It's a long way from Louisiana to the Penn State campus, but Penn State also is in the blood of his two sons. Even though Rich didn't push them, they wanted to play for Penn State.

Rich and Patricia Mauti's oldest son, Patrick, walked on, played sparingly—mostly on special teams—for three years, and then lettered in 2009. But behind the scenes Pat was one of the team leaders and helped take charge of the Penn State chapter of Lift for Life.

Michael, however, was a star linebacker in the making from the first time he played as a highly rated recruit in his freshman year, 2008. However, just as

Penn State and Nebraska players intermingle, kneel, and join hands at midfield in several minutes of silence to honor child sex-abuse victims before the kickoff of their game at Beaver Stadium on November 12, 2011. An emotionally drained Penn State team lost, 17–14. Photo courtesy of Mark Selders, Penn State University Intercollegiate Athletic Archives

medical problems hampered his father's career, two serious knee injuries forced Michael to miss the 2009 season and most of the 2011 season. He was on the sideline at the Nebraska game, as he had been all year, helping his younger teammates and doing whatever was asked of him by his coaches. His leadership ability and acumen would soar to the forefront in 2012. Rich, Patrick, and Michael are all part of the Penn State football legacy. And that legacy, as much as anything else, helped drive the 2012 team in its remarkable journey.

Rich Mauti's rallying of so many old players to the Nebraska game was a testament to that legacy. Under the circumstances of the child sex-abuse scandal, a large segment of the national media did not think the Nebraska game should be played.

I understood the need for more security, but I could not understand Tom Osborne's fear-stoking warning. Nebraska fans took it seriously, and many did not wear their red clothing. When the tailgating began in the shadow of the stadium, Nebraska fans quickly discovered Penn State fans to be friendly and gracious. The tailgating was quite subdued, which was not surprising, and many Nebraska fans said it was one of the friendliest football crowds they'd ever been around.

This fear of being attacked or harassed by rival fans because of the horrific criminal actions of one individual and the possible culpability of others is not only a sad commentary on college football but also on the insidious nature of a public and media that is quick to condemn and ostracize a significant segment of innocent people based on the real or perceived actions of a few.

Beaver Stadium was jammed with an announced crowd of 107,903, counting an unusual number of national media among the 600 credentialed for this game. It was sunny, with temperatures in the high 40s, and there were loud cheers when the seniors were introduced after the warm-ups. Shortly before noon, the players began their traditional entry through the tunnel near the dressing room in this nationally televised ESPN game. This time they were not running but walking, arm in arm, en masse toward the middle of the field. The cheering fans finally realized what was happening. From the other direction, the Nebraska players and their coaches were all walking toward the 50-yard line too. Soon they were in a circle, kneeling and holding hands, with their heads down in prayer. Outside the circle were more than 300 former Penn State football players who had showed up at the game to demonstrate their support and solidarity for the current team. Within moments the stadium was silent, and it remained quiet for a few minutes. When both teams stood up, the fans clapped heartily and then began cheering as the players went to the sidelines and the referees called the captains for the coin toss.

That was the most emotional moment in Penn State football history, and the saddest. I will never get it out of my mind. What Penn State and Nebraska did in that solemn five minutes brought out the best in college football.

Friday, November 18, 2011

Shortly after the team arrived at its Columbus hotel late Friday afternoon, the players were officially told the astonishingly bad news in a team meeting just before dinner—Joe Paterno had been diagnosed with a viral case of lung cancer.

My wife, Carole, and I were waiting near the hotel's back lobby area when the players arrived. We didn't know at the time that the players hadn't been told. We briefly talked to a couple of coaches and staffers, and they didn't say much. They didn't know any more than we did. I didn't learn the details of Paterno's diagnosis until returning to State College two days later, and I knew this was not going to end well.

En route to Columbus, Joe Paterno's son, Jay, told the football staff privately that Joe has been diagnosed with lung cancer. Some of the players also knew it once the plane landed, because of text messages and Twitter. Apparently the news was made public while the team's charter flight was in the air. Penn State fans are wondering how this will affect the players' attitudes and mental state for Saturday's game, especially with Jay on the coaching staff.

Saturday, November 19, 2011

Game Day: Penn State at Ohio State. Despite an 8–2 record and a No. 21 standing in the BCS rankings, the wounded Lions were a surprising 10-point underdog to the Buckeyes, who were struggling under an interim coach following the firing of Jim Tressel in the aftermath of serious NCAA violations. With the lights on for a 3:30 PM kickoff, Penn State went on the attack with a previously unseen wildcat offense featuring two running backs from the shotgun formation and took a 10–0 lead in the first quarter. A couple of field goals by Fera helped make the score 20–14 at the half, and that became the final result, thanks to a strong defense and Fera's punting.

You have to credit Tom Bradley and the coaches for keeping the team focused in light of the bad news about Paterno. Meeting with the media after the game, Bradley said he had told the players "to show a lot of character and resolve," adding, "I couldn't be prouder of them." Bradley also revealed that Jay Paterno had suggested using the wildcat formation, and Jay gave credit to his father, saying, "The old guy sitting at home is smiling."

The small contingent of Penn State fans leaving the stadium and tailgating in the parking lots were smiling too, not only because of the victory but also because of the unusual friendliness of the Ohio State fans. Outside of a couple isolated nasty remarks about Sandusky after the game, my wife and I neither heard nor saw anything malicious. That also seemed to be the sentiment of other Penn Staters who were there. Many heard nothing at all, and the leaders of Penn State's alumni association thanked Ohio State and its fans for their kindness during this embarrassing, awkward, and sensitive situation.

Monday, November 21, 2011

Louis Freeh, the former head of the FBI, was hired by the Penn State Board of Trustees to investigate the university's involvement in the Sandusky child-abuse allegations. Freeh told the media the board had given him total independence, saying, "I'm tasked with investigating the matter fully, fairly, and completely, without fear or favoritism."

At the time, this announcement was hardly noticed by the players on the 2011 team, but the result of Freeh's nearly eight-month-long investigation would have a more damaging impact on the 2012 team than anyone could have imagined.

Saturday, November 26, 2011

Game Day: Penn State at Wisconsin. For the first time since 1991, the last game of the regular season was played on Thanksgiving weekend, 700 miles from friendly Beaver Stadium and inside one of the most intimidating atmospheres in college football: Camp Randall Stadium. And with Penn State fans still concerned about how they would be treated because of the scandal, most of the traveling Nittany Nation stayed home and watched the game on television.

This was a battle for the Leaders Division title and the first-ever Big Ten Championship playoff game, and a trip to the Rose Bowl the following Saturday. Both teams were 9–2, but Wisconsin was made a whopping 15-point favorite. The outcome was much worse. Penn State jumped off to an early first-quarter 7–0 lead but never scored again as Wisconsin turned four turnovers into 24 points and routed the battered Nittany Lions 45–7. "No excuses," Bradley told reporters. "We just didn't play very well today in all phases of the game."

Carole and I decided before this season started not to go to today's game because of the Thanksgiving holiday, the logistics of travel, and the expense. We have some good friends in Madison who are involved with Wisconsin football in different ways, and this was the first time in a decade we missed getting together with them prior to the game. Of course, if Penn State had pulled off the major upset, we would have been figuratively kicking ourselves. Yet I am not surprised at the outcome. The pressure on each of the players and coaches, along with the national media criticism of Penn State football, finally reached the breaking point, and they collapsed.

But a 9–3 season despite all of the adversity they have been through is extraordinary. After today's game, Penn State has the fourth-best overall record in the Big Ten—after Wisconsin, Michigan State, and Michigan—and that should be enough for a good postseason bowl game. But even before today's game was played, many media critics and others were calling on Penn State to reject any bowl invitation or for the bowls to snub Penn State because of the scandal.

Bradley addressed these often-derogatory appeals in his postgame remarks, saying, "We have a group of players who didn't do anything. They worked their tails off. They deserve an opportunity to play a bowl game. They were not involved in this [scandal]."

Chapter 1

The Search

Monday, November 28, 2011

Acting athletics director Dave Joyner, a onetime All-American tackle and Academic All-American for Paterno, announced a five-person search committee "charged with identifying candidates and appointing" the next head football coach. Joyner was appointed committee chairman by new Penn State president Rodney Erickson, the former provost. The committee consisted of Linda Caldwell, Penn State faculty athletics representative; Charmelle Green, Penn State associate athletics director and senior woman administrator; Ira Lubert, a member of the board of trustees and chairman and cofounder of Independence Capital Partners and Lubert Adler Partners; Dr. John Nichols, emeritus professor, Penn State College of Communications, and chair of the Coalition on Intercollegiate Athletics; and Russ Rose, head coach of the Penn State women's volleyball team.

It was telling that Lubert was on the committee. Just three years before, Lubert was the principal benefactor when Penn State hired a new wrestling coach. Offering a salary that was far beyond what any college wrestling coach was then (or is now) receiving, Penn State hired the best, Cael Sanderson, away from his Iowa State alma mater. By the time the 2012–13 wrestling season was over, Sanderson's Nittany Lions team had shocked the wrestling world by winning three straight national championships—a feat no other East Coast team had ever done. In fact, the only one other team east of the Mississippi to win just one NCAA title is Minnesota. Penn State's football nation wondered if the university would be as fortunate in the selection of the next head football coach—a man who would affect the future not only of the football team but the university itself.

After considering some college coaches, it did not take long for the committee to throw in the names of some NFL coaches, including quarterbacks coach Tom Clements of Green Bay, who had played for Notre Dame, and Mike Munchak, the rookie head coach of the Tennessee Titans who had been a star guard for Paterno in the early 1980s and then had a Hall of Fame career with the Titans franchise in Houston.

Rumors continued to swirl for 34 day from the time the search committee was announced before the name of Bill O'Brien, offensive coordinator and quarterbacks coach of the New England Patriots, first surfaced. Many of Penn State's prominent former players were adamant and vocal in their support of a Penn State man and they favored Bradley or Munchak.

It was odd even to *have* a search committee for the position. "There were dozens of schools looking for head football coaches at the time," Nichols told me afterward, "and only two or three had search committees, and zero had faculty members on the committee. Usually the coach for revenue sports is hired by the athletics director and the president, with maybe a consultant involved, and for the other sports it's the athletics director and maybe the faculty rep with the president approving. To realize we had two faculty members is amazing, and we were not isolated. The committee worked well together."

This is the first time ever that a search committee has been formed to hire the head football coach at Penn State. He will be the 15th one since the first in 1892 and only the fifth since 1918. I find the committee an intuitive choice of people. The faculty representative is a natural choice, and Green, hired just five months ago from Notre Dame, gives the group an experienced administrator from the outside. Lubert is an influential member of the Penn State Board of Trustees, a wealthy donor, and a longtime friend of Joyner's, since they were teammates on the Penn State wrestling team in the early 1970s. Nichols has been one of the university's most respected faculty members, even in his supposed retirement—a leader in the faculty senate who has been an advocate of the coexistence of athletics within the strong academic environment, and he is also a longtime football season-ticket holder. Rose, already a Penn State and collegiate volleyball coaching legend with four national championship teams to his credit, is highly regarded for his keen mind, blunt honesty, intellect, and sense of humor. He also was friendlier with Paterno than most of the other head coaches in the athletics department.

What is highly unusual is having a search committee at all. This is standard for high positions in academia but rare for hiring head coaches in any sport—especially in sports that bring in revenue, such as football and men's and women's basketball.

Of course, the committee will only make the recommendation. Joyner will do the actual hiring, with the president's approval, and will handle the contract.

Rumors started even before the committee was formed. Will it be someone already on the staff? If so, the likely candidates are Bradley; linebacker coach Ron Vanderlinden, once the head coach at Maryland; or highly respected defensive line coach Larry Johnson. If not any of them, then perhaps an ultra-successful collegiate head coach elsewhere? Urban Meyer was mentioned as a Paterno successor starting months before the arrest of Sandusky and the firing of Paterno, and there were unconfirmed reports that Meyer met with President Spanier at one point. Other names being bandied about are Boise State's Chris Petersen, Mississippi State's Dan Mullen, and Utah's Kyle Whittingham.

The first two mandatory objectives of Penn State's new head coach will be to win over the players for 2012 and salvage what is becoming a shaky and unsuccessful recruiting outcome. Then he will need to win over the lettermen and the fans. Meanwhile, the 2011 team has one game remaining under interim coach Tom Bradley.

Sunday, December 4, 2011

Penn State was the seventh and next-to-last Big Ten team selected for a bowl game, in spite of its 9–3 record. Three of the teams they beat finished with worse records but were chosen ahead of them for better bowls. However, the good news was that the game, the two-year-old Ticket City Bowl, would be played in Dallas' historic Cotton Bowl stadium on January 2, the same day as five other bowls, including the Rose and Fiesta.

It was obvious that Penn State was passed over because of the Sandusky scandal, and the other bowls wanted to avoid the negative publicity. Except for the Penn State administration, neither the players nor the fans were happy about going to such a minor and obscure bowl game as the Ticket City Bowl. They should have felt fortunate to have been invited anywhere because of the media and public pressure to ignore the Lions completely. If the Ticket City Bowl had not selected Penn State, that would have left the Little Caesar's Pizza Bowl in Detroit against the champion of the MAC (Mid American Conference).

Dallas at noon on January 2 was a lot better than Detroit at 4:30 PM on Tuesday, December 27.

The players were especially bitter and complained publicly. Many did not want to play, and they argued with Joyner in an angry private team meeting when the acting athletics director tried to reason with them. After a few players-only meetings and discussions with the coaches, the team mood changed for the better as they practiced for the game.

However, the disappointment and tension remained, and it boiled over on Saturday, December 17, in an argument on the practice field between starting quarterback Matt McGloin and wide receiver Curtis Drake that led to a locker-room fight. McGloin suffered a concussion and faced disciplinary action. It was not what the team needed at this critical juncture.

With all the other games starting later than noon Eastern time, the start time set for the Ticket City Bowl, there should be a decent cable television audience on ESPNU. The matchup is a good one, with a high-scoring 12–1 Houston team that could have been in the BCS Sugar or Orange Bowls had they not been upset in the Conference USA Football Championship Game. Houston has been ranked No. 19 in the final BCS standings while Penn State is No. 22. And so the fledging bowl that was created to replace the famed Cotton Bowl game that moved to the Dallas Cowboys' new stadium is happy to host the teams, despite the controversy surrounding Penn State.

Sunday, December 11, 2011

In a televised game between the New England Patriots and the Washington Redskins, viewers were startled midway through the fourth quarter when they saw the Patriots offensive coordinator and quarterback coach, Bill

Bill O'Brien, offensive coordinator of the New England Patriots, seen here with quarterback Tom Brady and head coach Bill Belichick, made national headlines in an angry sideline confrontation with Brady during a game against the Redskins on December 11. But it was not until 20 days later that O'Brien's name was first brought up as the possible head coach of the Penn State football team.

Photo courtesy of AP Images

O'Brien, get into a fiery and intense face-to-face argument with All-Pro quarterback Tom Brady on the Patriots bench. Little did we Penn Staters who watched the video back then realize we were seeing our next head football coach.

Today's confrontation started when O'Brien stormed toward Brady, who was sitting on the bench after throwing an interception in the back of the Redskins end zone with the Patriots narrowly leading by seven points. The quarrel started slowly but exploded when Brady said something that angered O'Brien and they had to be bodily separated.

Later, after the Patriots won 34–27, they both apologized for the public tantrum. Brady admitted he was wrong, and O'Brien said, "It's just two competitive guys that want the best for the team." But within hours the video of their encounter had been seen by millions of people via television and the Internet, and the heretofore virtually unknown O'Brien has become famous as the man who challenged legendary quarterback Tom Brady. O'Brien told reporters he heard from his mother after the sideline incident, and she told him to watch his language.

Sunday, January 1, 2012

New Year's Day is the traditional day for the Rose Bowl Parade and the major postseason bowl games, but they were delayed by one day because of the final day of the NFL's regular season. It was a routine day for the Penn State football team, with a walk-through at the Cotton Bowl and team meals and meetings while also relaxing around the hotel and watching NFL games.

They heard and saw the same media reports as the public about their next head coach. Earlier in the week, a few Penn State beat writers had cited sources saying Tennessee Titans coach Mike Munchak had the job locked up. He had formally denied it Wednesday morning, December 29, but reports continued that the position was his if he wanted it. Bradley was out, the reports claimed, and Green Bay's Clements was second in line. Then on New Year's Eve, ESPN's college football reporter Joe Schad brought O'Brien and Greg Schiano of Rutgers into the conversation.

Early this morning, *USA Today*'s Jon Saraceno, a Penn State graduate, filed a brief item on the newspaper's website and via a tweet asserting, "only contract details need to be finalized before O'Brien is the man." A few hours later, ESPN's NFL insider Chris Mortensen and reporter Adam Schefter claimed O'Brien will sign a contract in the next week.

Naturally, the coaching rumors and the continuing scandal are the prime topics of conversation wherever Penn State fans gather here in Dallas. This is the smallest turnout by Penn Staters for a postseason game that I can remember, but there are plenty of loyal ones who I have been seeing at away games for the last few years. The main bar at the team hotel where many of them stayed, including my wife and me, was active but not as boisterous as it usually is when Penn Staters overwhelm the place during pre-bowl week.

Despite the circumstances, the fans and the players seem to be enjoying Dallas and the Hyatt Regency Hotel, which is just a short walking distance from the Kennedy assassination site and the historical district's restaurants and bars.

Carole and I, being longtime Pittsburgh Steelers fans, wanted to watch the Steelers-Browns game, but the hotel televisions were not carrying it. We had to find a sports bar a few blocks away where we could watch that game. We saw just three or four other fans wearing Penn State clothing inside. If this were a normal postseason bowl game for Penn State, the place would have been filled with Nittany Lions fans. Except for the waitress, hardly anyone else paid attention to us. So not everyone hates Penn State.

Monday, January 2, 2012

Game Day: Penn State vs. Houston in the Ticket City Bowl. The renovated Cotton Bowl stadium was half-empty when Penn State kicked off in sunny, 47-degree temperatures and the crowd, later announced at 46,817, was more subdued than those at most January 1 or 2 bowl games.

This was expected to be a tight battle between the Houston offense, averaging nearly 600 yards per game, and Penn State's strong defense, and that's the main reason Houston was a touchdown favorite. However, Penn State was playing without starting quarterback Matt McGloin, who was still recovering from his concussion resulting from his locker-room fight with Drake.

McGloin's absence was obvious from the start, with erratic sophomore Rob Bolden at quarterback, but it was also apparent that the Penn State players weren't into this game. The Lions' stilted defense couldn't handle Houston's up-tempo attack as the Cougars blitzed to a 17–0 first-quarter lead, made it 27–7 late in the third quarter, and went on to win 30–14. The final score was not surprising, and it could have been worse.

The outcome of the game was disappointing, but otherwise the players and fans enjoyed themselves. With such a sparse turnout of Penn State fans, my wife and I found ourselves sitting right on the 50-yard line for the first time ever at a Nittany Lions game—except for the times decades ago when I covered games from the press box.

The Houston crowd sitting to our left was gracious, and there weren't any problems with them related to Penn State's sex-abuse scandal. Apparently there were a couple of isolated incidents outside and inside the stadium, including the appearance of an individual dressed as Pedobear, which for many people is a symbol of pedophilia. Some in the media overreacted to the costumed bear and gave it more publicity than it deserved.

I continue to wonder about the responsibility—or lack thereof— of a large segment of the media since the initial arrest of Sandusky. This is not going to go away anytime soon. Certainly the man who becomes the next head coach must know what he is getting into and the national scrutiny he will be under. It is probably going to get worse than better for Penn State before it begins to turn around, and the football team is going to be ground zero for the rants made by the media and public.

Today I thought about the football team and how it will be different too, with perhaps an entirely new coaching staff with new ideas and new concepts that might be radically different from what the Penn State football nation has known for the last 46 years. Tom Bradley had similar thoughts, and after today's game promised reporters the Penn State offense will change in 2012 whether he or someone else is the head coach: "Next year we'll have a totally different look on offense one way or another."

What exactly that means is still a mystery. When questioned about the O'Brien rumors by beat writers at a pep rally at the Cotton Bowl before the game, Joyner said, "There is no deal in place with anybody."

Chapter 2

The Torch Is Passed

Wednesday, January 4, 2012

On Tuesday, January 3, Mike Munchak officially removed his name as a possible candidate for Penn State's head coaching position at a season-ending Tennessee Titans news conference. Some media reported that Munchak was never formally interviewed.

Related, multiple media reports said the hiring of Bill O'Brien as Penn State's next head football coach was imminent. Sources told ESPN, *USA Today*, the *Pittsburgh Post-Gazette*, and others that the Patriots' offensive coordinator would meet with Penn State officials the next day, Thursday, to finalize and sign the contract.

Saturday, January 7, 2012

With the Patriots getting a bye in the first week of NFL playoff games, Bill O'Brien was formally introduced as the 15th head football coach in Penn State history at a late-morning nationally televised news conference in the ballroom of the Nittany Lion Inn on campus. The crowd of about 300 included not only the media but also many people from the athletics department and some members

Penn State fans give a standing ovation to new head football coach Bill O'Brien; his wife, Colleen; and their six-year-old son Michael during a break in a late-afternoon basketball game a day after O'Brien's hiring was formally announced at a morning news conference on January 7. Photo courtesy of Mark Selders, Penn State University Intercollegiate Athletic Archives

of the board of trustees and search committee. O'Brien was introduced by acting athletics director Dave Joyner and president Rodney Ericson, who told the gathering, "We found the right man to lead our football program. He's a person of great integrity, leadership, and skill."

O'Brien's wife, Colleen; six-year-old son, Michael; and one of his two brothers, Tom, were sitting in the front row. Michael was wearing a blue Penn State jersey with the No. 25, the numeral of the Lions' outstanding sophomore running back Silas Redd. O'Brien referred briefly to his nine-year-old son, Jack, who was not there, but it was not until the formal news conference was long over that the media and public who were watching learned that Jack has a rare developmental disability in the brain called lissencephaly. They also learned O'Brien and his wife are dedicated to Jack.

O'Brien's five-year contract was released to the media, guaranteeing the coach $2.3 million annually with a base annual salary starting at $950,000 per year with a yearly 5 percent increase, $1 million additional compensation each year for radio and television programs produced by Penn State and a reasonable number of public appearances, and $350,000 per year from Nike for speaking engagements and the use of Nike athletic apparel by the football team. Among the other perks, including the use of an automobile, O'Brien also could earn up to another $200,000 annually for winning a Big Ten division and conference title, the BCS championship, and taking the team to a postseason bowl game.

This was the first time the media and the public had been officially told how much money was being paid to the head football coach and had the full contract available to read. Paterno's salary and other contract compensation were never disclosed, although they have been reported to as similar to O'Brien's.

After the conference, most of the local media that covers Penn State football were impressed by what they had heard from O'Brien.

Neil Rudel of the *Altoona Mirror*, the senior man covering Penn State going back to 1977 but now the paper's managing editor and a sports columnist, wrote: "If Bill O'Brien's hiring wasn't the proverbial big-name grand slam for which Nittany Lions fans were hoping, Penn State's new football coach clearly hit the ball way out of the park during an introductory press conference Saturday. Now, if he can coach and recruit as well as he talks, the Nittany Nation will be quite pleased."

NO QUESTION: O'BRIEN RIGHT CHOICE, blared the headline in the *Reading Eagle* story by Rich Scarcella, the longest-tenured daily beat writer, who started covering Penn State football in 1989.

"O'Brien displayed a strong air of confidence in his abilities without coming across in any way shape or form an arrogant personality," wrote Phil Grosz, publisher of *Blue White Illustrated*, which has been covering Penn State athletics since 1980. He continued, "Not only did O'Brien indicate to me he wants to put on the field a championship caliber football team, but he is already fully aware of the student/athlete tradition that was established by Paterno over the past 46 years here at Penn State."

However, some in the national media wasn't as convinced or as kind.

A day before O'Brien's news conference, Pat Forde of Yahoo Sports wrote: "...the school reportedly is hiring a career assistant with an undistinguished collegiate record off a [Patriots] staff that has produced notable head-coaching failures (Charlie Weis at Notre Dame, Romeo Crennel at Cleveland, Josh McDaniels at Denver). If recruits are galvanized by this hire, it would be a surprise."

Nicholas Goss, a young columnist for BleacherReport.com working out of Boston, claimed, "Bill O'Brien is a terrible hire for Penn State because he has no prior head coaching experience at either the NFL or collegiate level, and he's also another overrated Bill Belichick coordinator.... O'Brien will fail mightily under the intense pressure and close watch on the program by the media and fans. He is not going to be able to handle the kind of expectations that await him at Penn State."

Whether previous experience as a head coach is necessary is always a matter of opinion. Other assistants from the outside have taken over major programs with the same criticism but never under the cloud of a notorious scandal. On paper, O'Brien had nearly as much experience as Paterno when the latter became the head coach in 1966, and O'Brien's background was more diversified. Paterno spent 17 years as a Lions assistant until being promoted. O'Brien had 15 years with nine coaching assignments at Brown, Georgia Tech, Maryland, and Duke and five years with the Patriots, rising from a lowly offensive assistant with mundane tasks to the offensive coordinator and quarterback coach. He also was three years older than Paterno on the day he became the head coach.

Fran Fisher and I were at today's news conference, sitting in the last row of seats in front of the TV cameras and chatting intermittently throughout, as usual. O'Brien's first words as he looked at the large audience bathed by the bright television lights were, "This is unbelievable." Fran and I were quite impressed with O'Brien's poise, intelligence, and confidence. He has an engaging personality and a sense of humor too. At one time referring to his premature baldness, he joked, "I look like I'm 50, but I'm only 42—follicularly challenged." He seemed fully prepared for every question and more, and never once referred to any notes.

"I'm not here to be Joe Paterno," O'Brien said. "There's only one Joe Paterno. There will never be enough words to say what he did for this program. It's [now] my job as the head football coach at Penn State to have the best football program both on and off the field." Because he is a Brown graduate and football player as Paterno was three decades before, he said he has always admired Paterno and what Paterno has accomplished.

O'Brien later reiterated how much he respects Paterno and Penn State. "I grew up following the Penn State football program," he said. "I was the type of person who liked to watch them because of the [white] helmets, because of the [plain] uniforms, the black cleats, no names on the backs of the jerseys."

Most members of the search committee were at the news conference to visibly show their support for the decision. John Nichols told me O'Brien's name had come up early and he kept rising in the evaluations. "We had many candidates," Nichols said. "Contrary to what a lot of people thought and what some reporters wrote, Penn State was not toxic. Some of the biggest names in coaching expressed strong interest, and we had serious interviews with some of them. When all is said and done, O'Brien was far and away the committee's top choice, and our recommendation was unanimous."

O'Brien took questions for 32 minutes, saying he will continue his coaching with the Patriots through the playoffs and through the Super Bowl if necessary, but he will be dividing his time with Penn State. He said he will begin immediately to hire the best staff to fit his program, and he surprised the audience when he said defensive line coach Larry Johnson will stay on the football staff and be immediately assigned to coordinate the ongoing recruiting that is down to the crucial stage of player signings.

O'Brien declined to talk about the scandal but did acknowledge he will deal with it. He's also aware of the discontentment within the Penn State family about hiring an outsider. He told the audience, "I understand that there's some controversy out there right now. I can see it. I understand that. I am in charge of this [football] family right now…. I'm a pretty mentally tough guy…. I feel like I can do this and lead this program…I can't wait to get going and get everyone headed in the right direction…"

O'Brien told reporters he has written a letter to all the football lettermen asking for their trust and support. He said it took him two nights to compose. The essence of the letter is best summed up by the last two sentences: "You are why we want to be here. We want you to know that you will always be welcome as a part of our program, because we are Penn State."

Even before the formal news conference began, a few prominent lettermen began publicly rallying support for O'Brien, including Blackledge and the normally reclusive two-time All-American linebacker Shane Conlan. Apparently Conlan, Blackledge, and a number of other lettermen, including the outgoing and incoming presidents of the influential Penn State Lettermen's Club—Tim Sweeney and Justin Kurpeikis, respectively—had met or spoken to O'Brien by telephone a few days before today's conference.

"I was impressed during our conversation," Blackledge told reporters, "by his passion, his values, the respect and understanding of Penn State football he possessed, and his enthusiasm about leading the program in the future."

Conlan said, "He has great knowledge of the tradition and history of Penn State football.... He has great presence and leadership qualities and it was easy to tell he is committed.... I am going to support Coach O'Brien and the program any way I can. I think Bill will do a great job."

After the news conference, O'Brien went off for some interviews with local TV reporters and then returned to take more questions, just off the podium, from the cluster of reporters for almost another half hour. He didn't back away when some of the questions became a little testy, and he is definitely a confident man in control.

And just as he was hustled away from the few remaining reporters hovering around him, he answered one last question with a smile: "No, we are not changing the uniforms."

It will be impossible for O'Brien to match all of Paterno's accomplishments. Whatever success he is going to attain after this historic day will be up to him, his assistant coaches, and, most important of all, his players. And the players returning from the

2011 team are uptight and wary about the coaching change and the continuing reverberations from the Sandusky scandal.

Sunday, January 8 to Sunday, February 5, 2012

O'Brien spent a hectic four weeks meeting the demands and responsibilities of his two high-profile jobs. New England advanced through the playoffs to the Super Bowl in Indianapolis, and O'Brien flew back and forth from State College and Boston by private plane in a whirlwind schedule. Before leaving Sunday night, January 8, O'Brien met with his new Penn State players for the first time in a candid 45-minute session, and they, too, were impressed, according to media reports:

— Linebacker Michael Mauti: "I'm excited about working with him. I could run through the wall right now."

— Center Matt Stankiewitch: "He's a great fit for a Penn State man. Honest, respectable, a lot of charisma."

— Running Back Silas Redd: "I'll tell you right now, all the guys that were in that squad room are behind him and ready to rally behind him no matter what."

O'Brien also told the players that linebackers coach Ron Vanderlinden would stay on. *The (Nashville) Tennessean* also reported Sunday night that the Titans' offensive quality-control coach, Charles London, would be O'Brien's running backs coach. But neither position was confirmed officially until two days later.

Before the end of the week, O'Brien had eight men on his staff, and except for Johnson and Vanderlinden, all of them had some tie to O'Brien in his previous coaching jobs. The others were: Ted Roof, defensive coordinator, who had the same position at Auburn the three previous years; Mac McWhorter, offensive line, who came out of a one-year retirement after spending nine seasons at Texas; Stan Hixon, assistant head coach and wide receivers coach, who had been the Buffalo Bills' wide receivers coach for the last two seasons; John Butler, secondary, most recently South Carolina's special teams coach; and John Strollo, tight ends, offensive line coach at Ball State in 2011.

A little more than a week later, another South Carolina staffer, Craig Fitzgerald, who had worked with O'Brien when they were at Maryland and played tight end for Maryland from 1994 to 1996, was named the director of strength and conditioning for football. It took even longer for O'Brien to find the right men to be his trainer and quarterbacks coach, and neither one had a direct connection to O'Brien. However, Ted Bream, trainer of the Chicago Bears for 19 years, who was named director of athletic training services on February 11, was a Penn State graduate and an assistant trainer on Penn State's 1982 national championship team. Bream was a longtime friend of Fitzgerald's. They were classmates at Philadelphia's La Salle College High School, and after graduating in 1991 they were in each other's weddings. Then on February 17, O'Brien told reporters that Charlie Fisher, who had spent nine seasons at Vanderbilt before moving to Miami of Ohio in 2011, would be his quarterbacks coach.

I am not familiar with any of O'Brien's new hires, but they have some impressive collegiate and NFL credentials with Roof, McWhorter, and Hixon once coaching teams that won national championships at Auburn, Texas, and LSU, respectively. I am as pleased as most Penn State fans that O'Brien will retain Johnson and Vanderlinden. They have been responsible for six of the last eight Penn State first-team All-Americans, and either one might have been selected as the head coach under different circumstances.

The only controversy seems to settle around the weight-training program. Fitzgerald is a proponent of the free-weight, or volume, system while his predecessor, J.T. Thomas, who had been in charge since 1991, believes in high-intensity training. I don't know much about the two schools of thought, but that they are polar opposites. The regimen and exercises are drastically different, and the debate is often heated over which one is best for football players. But collegiate and professional teams utilize both programs. No doubt, this will be a severe change for the Penn State players, and we shall see how well they adapt.

Sunday, January 22, 2012

Joe Paterno died at 9:25 AM today in Mount Nittany Hospital. Paterno's death from complications of lung cancer is not a surprise, because there have been media reports since before Christmas that his health has been deteriorating. His passing has sent shock waves across the Nittany Nation because it happened so quickly after his firing and with his national image in tatters from the fallout since the Sandusky grand jury presentment.

O'Brien said he called Paterno the day after his initial news conference, but because of his frenzied schedule and Paterno's illness, he never had a chance to follow up with a personal visit. O'Brien met Paterno when he was a senior at Brown in 1992, and he still has a photograph of that now-historic meeting.

Tuesday, January 24 to Thursday, January 26, 2012

Three days of mourning started with Paterno's closed casket lying in state for a day at the Pasquerilla Spiritual Center, across the street from the Pattee-Paterno Library. The casket was guarded by dozens of his former players, taking shifts, while Paterno's family greeted nearly 40,000 people who passed by—close friends, acquaintances, hundreds of football lettermen and their wives, and thousands of everyday students and fans who stood in line for hours in the cold, damp weather to honor the man nicknamed "JoePa."

Bill O'Brien and the 2012 team were among the first to pay their respects when the private viewing started early on Tuesday, January 24, and O'Brien met Joe's wife, Sue Paterno, for the first time. The team was followed by some 800 of Paterno's former players and their wives, lettermen from an earlier vintage, ex-coaches, and other special guests. Most of them had to wait in line for one to two hours in the cold.

Afterward, the lettermen packed the expansive Recruiting Lounge and Letterman's Lounge in Beaver Stadium, right above the media room and locker room, for a wake, telling stories to each other about Paterno, his idiosyncrasies, and his trademark squeaky voice. O'Brien went there while many lettermen were still in line at the viewing and personally introduced himself to as many as he could and then spoke for several minutes to the large crowd that already had gathered. What he told the lettermen was private, but several later said that he spoke of his respect for Paterno and the Penn State program, and he asked them to be behind him as he continued to build Penn State football on the foundation Paterno created.

Eight days later, in a teleconference from Indianapolis, O'Brien told the Penn State beat reporters he was determined to lead the team through the viewing for Paterno "to make sure that the guys understood how I felt about [Joe's passing].... It was an emotional time for everybody involved at Penn State. We lost a great man. We lost a great coach. We lost somebody that was huge in the coaching profession as far as I'm concerned personally for what he meant to college football and coaching in general, but more importantly our players lost a man that recruited them, was their coach, was a father figure to many of those guys.... I flew back to New England and they continued on.... I was very impressed with how our team handled themselves throughout the three days paying tribute to Coach Paterno."

Thanks to three of Paterno's former assistant coaches—Fran Ganter, Dick Anderson, and Dan Radakovich—Carole and I were invited to join the lettermen and their wives at the viewing and the wake at Beaver Stadium. However, by the time we arrived, O'Brien was in the process of leaving to catch his flight back to Boston. But he stopped a few minutes in the lobby of the Penn State All-Sports Museum to talk to each of us, and my wife, meeting him for the first time, was impressed. "Young guy, new blood," she told me.

Wednesday, January 25, 2012

A private funeral for Paterno was followed by a long procession past Beaver Stadium and through downtown State College as crowds clogged the streets to wave good-bye. Television stations throughout Pennsylvania, along with ESPN and the Big Ten network, broadcast much of the motorcade live to hundreds of thousands, but the private burial was not broadcast.

Thursday, January 26, 2012

More than 13,000 jammed the Bryce Jordan Center for a two-and-a-half-hour nationally televised, semipublic memorial service for Paterno that included homages and tributes from family, former players, Nike founder Phil Knight, and then-current player Michael Mauti. The mourners included Big Ten commissioner Jim Delany, Ohio State's then-new football coach Urban Meyer, Iowa's football coach Kirk Ferentz, and Michigan's former coach Lloyd Carr. "I came from a Penn State family," Mauti told the gathering. "My dad, Rich, played here. My brother, Patrick, played here. I always heard what Coach Paterno meant.... Speaking on behalf of the current team right now, this has been a tough time for all of us. I just want to thank everybody. These lettermen have set the bar for what it means to have success with honor, and that is our job now, to continue on throughout this decade and the decades to come to uphold that tradition."

There might have been twice as many people or more inside the Bryce Jordan Center today if it was bigger and open to the public. For this service, tickets distributed by the athletics department were required. Carole and I sat among the lettermen, and I saw many familiar faces. We felt honored to be there.

We were there early, so I had a chance to talk to several of Joe's former players. Sitting behind us were Charlie Pittman and his son, Tony, who were both Academic All-Americans. I covered Charlie during Paterno's early seasons in the late 1960s, when Charlie became Paterno's first All-American running back, and we have become friends in the last decade. Charlie was one of the 12 speakers, representing the teams from the '60s, and he talked about being Paterno's first African American recruit, telling the audience: "Joe made his program his second family…. Rest in peace, Coach. We'll take it from here."

Despite the large crowd, it was an emotional service, with a lot of tears, tributes, and laughs as the players told jokes about their beloved coach and his idiosyncrasies. As everyone was slowly filing out of the Bryce Jordan Center, I thought about the finality of what had just happened. Joe is now part of history. He will always be in our hearts, but his era has ended. Then I remembered the title of a memorial book produced by the Associated Press shortly after the assassination of President Kennedy and the sad and traumatic weeklong national mourning: *The Torch Is Passed.*

Chapter 3

There's a New Sheriff in Town

Tuesday, January 24, 2012, Pt. 2

On the job for just one day, Craig Fitzgerald, Penn State's new strength-and-conditioning coach, surprised the team on Monday by ordering them to report early the next morning for a 5:30 AM hourlong workout outside in 32-degree temperatures. The players could not believe it, and neither could the fans when they learned about it. What no one realized was that these 5:30 AM winter drills would become routine in the new coaching regime of Bill O'Brien, every Tuesday and Friday until the beginning of spring practice.

O'Brien had told the players in his initial meeting with them that the first priority for Penn State football was to become a mentally tough team that would go all out in practice and in games, an "ironman" type of team that wouldn't be deterred by the unexpected or cold or rotten weather. Fitzgerald's first workout was just the start. A lot of things were going to be different from then on, whether players liked it or not, and they'd better get used to it.

Longtime observers of Penn State football cannot remember such an outside drill this early, even in the warmer temperatures of late

Michael Zordich jumps headfirst over a hurdle in one of Craig Fitzgerald's innovate drills at an early morning workout in near-freezing temperatures. Fitzgerald's new and surprising 7:00 AM workouts became a standard part of winter training for the 2012 team. Photo courtesy of Joe Hermitt, *(Harrisburg) Patriot-News*

spring and summer. Before the team's indoor practice complex, Holuba Hall, opened in 1986, Penn State had to work out outdoors to prepare for postseason bowl games, but it was never this early in the morning. Equally surprising, this is also the day the players will pay their respects to their former coach, and they are due at the chapel at 9:00 AM for the viewing.

Perhaps this outdoor drill on this specific day and at this precise time was to act like a shock treatment given to a mental patient. The players are still trying to cope with the Sandusky allegations; the firing of their legendary coach and his death that quickly followed; the abuse still being heaped on them by much of the media and public simply because they play for Penn State; and the uncertainty of their futures now in the hands of a man they hardly know. Today's drill was probably just what they needed to get them refocused.

Wednesday, February 1, 2012

For just the second time in Penn State history, a news conference was held to discuss recruiting on National Signing Day.

In the last two decades recruiting of high school players has developed into a public phobia. An entire new business has been created, including recruiting services using the Internet, magazines, television, and sports talk radio that turns unknowns into popular personalities deemed recruiting experts, with prominent recruits announcing their commitments on live television.

Recruiting talk was taboo for Penn State football until 2005, when the No. 1 recruit in the country, all-around athlete Derrick Williams of Greenbelt, Maryland, committed to Penn State in a live TV broadcast nearly two months before signing day and enrolled in the university in January. Then on signing day of 2005, Penn State issued a press release that included an unusual Internet link to a *New York Times* story on the recruiting class.

That fall, Williams and other members of his freshman class, including a preferred walk-on named Deon Butler of Woodbridge, Virginia, helped turn around a slide of four losing seasons in the last five years and take the 2005 team to victory in the Orange Bowl and a No. 3 ranking in the nation. So on the next signing day in 2006, Paterno held a news conference. But in the ensuing five years, Penn State has issued a simple news release on signing day, with a list of the signees but no accompanying bios or quotes from coaches or online sources.

This year the news conference was a teleconference with O'Brien because he is in Indianapolis, where the Patriots are preparing for their Super Bowl game against the New York Giants on Sunday. The media gathered in the Lasch Building, and after the teleconference was over, Penn State distributed a comprehensive press release with details about the new signees, and made assistant coaches available for interviews.

O'Brien was on the telephone line for 30 minutes and told reporters recruiting "really went really well" and credited assistant coach Larry Johnson for keeping everyone together through the transition. Penn State signed 19 players, but six other players decommitted after the Sandusky scandal broke. O'Brien praised Silas Redd, who, during the recruiting period, called every recruit who committed and thanked them. O'Brien also thanked the recruits for making their decision during these emotional times: "You've got to give these guys a lot of credit. They committed to Penn State University, they committed to the special place it is, where you can play football and get a degree. That was a testament to their mental toughness, their ability to stick it out."

Midway through the teleconference, while answering a question, O'Brien said something about the type of player he wants on his 2012 team and in the future:

"...a Penn State football player is...a smart, tough, instinctive player, with mental toughness and physical toughness, is going to come in [here] and do the right thing on and off the field. He's going to go to class. He's going to work hard in the classroom. He's going to come into that building and work very hard to be the best football player he can be. He's going to be a guy that accepts whatever role we ask him to accept and put the team first."

Friday, February 17, 2012

Another first. The media was invited to attend one of Craig Fitzgerald's 5:30 AM workouts on the practice field alongside the Lasch Building. The temperature was 37 degrees with a wind that made it seem colder, and the 20-some reporters and camera crews were bundled up. The players were wearing various layers of clothing, and at least one was wearing a partial ski mask. The media was amazed by what they saw. Fitzgerald was wearing just a T-shirt, shorts, a baseball cap, football shoes, and a whistle around his neck as he and O'Brien ran the players through a fast-paced series of intense, often challenging drills with heavy metal music blaring in the background. It was an eerie sight under the arc lights.

Near the end zone was an obstacle course where players had to vault over a three-foot hurdle and then belly flop on a blue gym mat. On another part of the field, players faced off one-on-one in an eight-foot circle outlined by orange tubing, and they wrestled all-out, WWE style. There were sprint drills, up-and-down drills (where a player hits the ground with his stomach, does a push-up, and jumps back up) and jumping drills.

Near the end of the hour, before sunrise, Fitzgerald whistled for everyone to gather at the 5-yard line for what he called "the Tug." Fitzgerald held up a blue disc with handles on opposing ends. He divided the group into offense and defense, and each side selected five players to go one-on-one. The offensive player tried to pull the disc over the goal line while the defensive player pulled toward the 10-yard line. With loud cheering and wisecracks from their teammates, the offense won 3–2, and the losing defense had to do five up-and-downs. All through the frantic workout, the players seemed enthused, having fun if not thoroughly enjoying themselves.

As equipment manager Spider Caldwell told me later, when the drills started, the players were quite vocal in wondering, "Who is this crazy guy?" They quickly learned Fitzgerald is an unusual character who loves being around the players, and outside of O'Brien, he may have the best relationship with all of the players except for each individual's position coach.

As the practice ended, O'Brien huddled the players around him, reminding them of a team meeting at 3:00, and then had Silas Redd take over. "It's on us, it's on us," Redd shouted to his teammates. "It's on us to carry this team."

The players strode into the weight-training room, and Fitzgerald gave the media a tour of the revamped facility. All the machines were gone, and the nearly empty room looked bigger, with seven power racks evenly spaced at one end and dumbbell racks lining the wall at the opposite end. With 17 additional power racks soon to be added, Fitzgerald explained, the entire team would be able to lift together, unlike in the past, when players had to take shifts on the machines.

The concept of these group workouts would come to represent the larger motif of team unity. O'Brien began using the words "One Team" in talking to the players, and he turned the phrase into the team motto. The athletics department's marketing group picked up on the motto and started using it too. The team now shouts "One Team!" at the end of each practice, before each game, and at other times too. T-shirts have been sold with those words printed on the front, and when a DVD of the video highlights of the unforgettable 2012 season went on sale in December, it was appropriately titled *One Team*.

I could not attend the 5:30 AM workout today because Carole and I were visiting our oldest daughter and her husband, Vicki and Jeff Rearick, in the much warmer temperatures of Jupiter, Florida. I read about what occurred in the numerous articles posted online by Penn State's beat reporters, and I also watched a couple of the videos they posted (see the appendix).

I've since learned that Fitzgerald arrives in the locker room at 3:30 AM on these frigid workout days, and equipment manager Spider Caldwell; Kirk Diehl, the coordinator of practice facilities; and some of their student managers are not far behind him.

It's apparent that what I have begun calling Fitzgerald's Friday Frigid Follies and the concept of the entire team training together in the strength room is the foundation of O'Brien's philosophy of team solidarity—working together in every facet off and on the field for the betterment of the team. The team comes first, not any single individual, and each player has to be loyal to that belief for O'Brien's team, in college or the NFL, to be successful.

Friday, February 17 to Sunday, February 19, 2012

O'Brien and many players made appearances at Penn State's famous THON charity dance marathon that raises money for pediatric cancer patients. The Penn State dance marathon is the world's largest student-run philanthropy, and since its start in 1977 it has raised nearly $102 million as of the end of the 2013 46-hour event. In 2012 O'Brien even went on the stage to speak at midnight to help boost the morale of the more than 700 student dancers on the floor of the Bryce Jordan Center. On Saturday afternoon O'Brien, 40 players, and some assistant coaches entertained a special group of 25 children who were pediatric cancer patients or survivors and their families as part of the marathon and Make-A-Wish program. The group was given a tour of the Lasch football building and then gathered in the players' lounge for an ice cream and cookies social and autograph session.

"This means a lot to these [players]," O'Brien told the group after three cheers of "We Are…Penn State!" by the children and their families. He said, "Raising money for this cause and raising money for the families that need help and also raising money to help find a cure for this horrible disease is what's really important to us on this weekend…. I'm really thrilled that you're here in our building, and I'm thrilled to be the head coach…. And to everyone that's here today, we're going to work very hard, every day and every hour of the day, to make you proud of this football team…and we feel we have the makings of what could possibly be a good football team."

In one respect, the 2012 THON not only raised money for a great cause but also helped bond a grieving and shaken Penn State community still trying to overcome the ignominy heaped upon it by the media and public for having a serial child molester in their midst for decades.

The football team has traditionally been involved with THON. This year was special for many reasons, and it is important to note that O'Brien had another important event on his mind when he took time out to talk to the group and sign autographs. Just down the hall from the players' lounge, more than 40 high school recruits were in the squad room meeting with other coaches and school administrators. The 2012 season is important, but so is the future.

Thursday, March 1, 2012

After nearly two months with Bill O'Brien as the head coach, Penn State football had changed visibly, and the media and fans were beginning to notice. The most obvious to everyone was players had started wearing caps and hats inside buildings. One of Joe Paterno's cardinal rules was no hats of any kind indoors, including ball caps in the Lasch locker room, and he would even make former players take off their hats whenever he saw them inside a building. Paterno's rules for players, coaches, and male staff also included no beards, moustaches, long hair, or earrings. O'Brien eliminated those bans too. And for the first time, players were permitted to wear bandanas, do-rags, and trooper hats with flaps during the conditioning drills.

There would be more policy changes ahead, particularly one the team wouldn't see until the fall when they traveled to away games: the coats and ties that Paterno made the players wear on road trips were replaced by informal traveling warm-ups.

Nothing specific to write about today, but I'm seeing some changes on the Penn State team. Perhaps they are generational things. Paterno was from a more genteel age, when taking off hats indoors and opening doors for women were in fashion. I, too, grew up in that polite environment, and I still don't like seeing men or boys wearing hats indoors, nor women wearing ball caps, especially in restaurants. Once, while in Lasch a few years ago, I absentmindedly left my Penn State ball cap on and heard the unmistakable squeaky voice of Paterno behind me: "Hey, Prato, get that hat off. You know better."

As for facial and long hair, I grew a beard in the early 1970s, and Carole still doesn't like it. But facial hair and long hair have been with us for thousands of years. If your job or marriage depends on the prohibition of hair, you bear with it or find a new job or wife.

Men wearing earrings is in style in the modern generation, and so are tattoos, and college and pro football players are among the leading practitioners of both. One of my three grandsons and two of my step-grandsons have tattoos, and a couple of them occasionally wear a tiny ring on their ear, but I have no intention to follow their lead. Then again, maybe a small tattoo visible on my right arm might be fitting if it had the words WE ARE...PENN STATE!

Bill O'Brien is young enough to be my son and the father for most of his players, so I completely understand why he and other coaches are more permissive than my generation. As for his rescinding of the hat policy, he told the media, "I wear a hat inside, and if I wear one, I can't forbid my players from doing it." And he admitted one reason he wears a hat indoors is that he's partially bald.

What the fans usually don't see but the media does is the severe organizational permutation going on within the confines of Lasch. Today a returning visitor who has not been in the football complex since the first of the year would see few familiar faces, not just in the coaches' offices but in the inner sanctum on the second floor.

Today Mike Poorman of StateCollege.com wrote about what's happening in a revealing column titled "Penn State Football: 55 Changes in the First 55 Days of the Bill O'Brien Era." The most publicized behind-the-scene change is the abrupt dismissal of Guido D'Elia, the director of communications and branding for football, whose numerous innovative marketing techniques helped turn once-sedate Beaver Stadium on game day into a roaring, intimidating madhouse that *Sports Illustrated* named "the Greatest Show in College Football." Not only was D'Elia fired, but the company he partially owned that produced the popular weekly syndicated TV program *The Penn State Football Story* during the football season was canceled as well.

Among the other changes listed by Poorman are: the reassignment of "the head coach's secretary out of the football office…same with the director of football operations…[and] the chief videographer left." Poorman also cites policy changes that were more helpful to the media than in the Paterno regime, including inviting the media to the 5:30 AM conditioning practice, "media interviews with the head coach, individually and in groups, in the off-season, PR people calling reporters to offer coaches for interviews, video interviews with the assistant coaches posted online, and [making] players… available—often—for in-person interviews."

O'Brien and his staff have also compiled a policy book of about 80 to 90 pages that includes job descriptions for players and staff and spring practice schedules. The new sheriff in town means business.

Chapter 4

It Happens Every Spring

Monday, March 26, 2012

On the first day of spring practice, Coach Bill O'Brien made his initial appearance in the Beaver Stadium media room at 1:30 PM to meet with reporters and then surprised them by inviting the group to the Lasch practice field at 4:30 to watch the last hour of practice. That was another departure from the Paterno era, when all practices—spring, preseason, or fall—were off-limits. O'Brien said quarterback was his main priority. He said he may not name a starter until the opening game against Ohio University, and the position was wide-open with veterans fifth-year senior Matt McGloin, junior Rob Bolden, and redshirt sophomore Paul Jones, who, O'Brien said, was starting off "with a clean slate."

As Dave Jones of the *Patriot-News* wrote three weeks later, as the competition intensified, "That QB situation is what particularly intrigues PSU fans about the new [coach]. Can Bill O'Brien, former position coach of Tom Brady, affect significant improvement in any one of the Lions' three quarterback candidates?"

Bolden had been Paterno's starter from his first game as a true freshman in 2010, with McGloin his backup—until McGloin replaced him in the seventh game of last season. Jones was one of the nation's highly recruited scholastic quarterbacks, just as Bolden was that same year. Jones was redshirted as a freshman and sat out all last season because of his academics, and he is still awaiting his final grades for this semester to become eligible in the fall.

O'Brien said he has not watched much game video of the quarterbacks or of the entire offense: "I didn't want to make any judgments on what they did on the football field...with not really knowing what they were doing scheme-wise offensively... and not really knowing how they were coaching it.... To this point I've been very pleased with these [quarterbacks]. They're competitive guys, they're smart guys. They really want to be coached. They want to be good." Although O'Brien's forte is coaching quarterbacks, he said Charlie Fisher will coach them, and he will call the plays on game day, with defensive coordinator Ted Roof concentrating on the defensive alignments. O'Brien also told the reporters tight ends will be a significant part of the offense, but the cornerstone will be running, just as it was with the New England Patriots.

Asked about Michael Mauti, who missed most of 2011 because of an ACL injury, O'Brien said Mauti won't participate in contact drills. He said, "He definitely, obviously is one of the core players on this football team, both from his leadership and from his work ethic, his family." O'Brien said he will need several leaders: "I'm not going to mention any guys specifically. There are definitely older guys on this team that have played a lot of football, and so we're hoping that those guys take some leadership roles. Leadership comes in a lot of different forms. Some guys don't say a word and they just lead by example. Some guys do both."

The competition at quarterback is not only the primary focus for O'Brien and his staff but also for the fans, and the fans seem to be favoring Jones. He was the sensation of the 2010 Blue-White game, the annual scrimmage that marks the end of spring practice and draws upward of 76,500 spectators. Bolden's performance deteriorated over the past two seasons, and McGloin has been hot and cold, winning games with bold plays and losing them with ill-advised passes that have led to many interceptions.

All Jones needs, many fans have said out loud, is a good quarterbacks coach. They don't know much about Fisher, but they are confident that O'Brien will be as instrumental as anyone in molding and determining Penn State's starting quarterback for 2012.

Tuesday, March 27 to Friday, April 20, 2012

As the 2012 Penn State football team worked its way through spring drills—15 practice and meeting days in a five-week span—the media got more access to practices and formal scrimmages as well as to players and coaches for interviews. As a result, fans learned more about what went on in spring practice than they had in years. This is a synopsis of what was being reported:

O'Brien was developing an up-tempo offense with NFL-like formations and tendencies and a more creative, diverse, and complex offensive playbook with the integration of three tight ends and the fullback. Tailback Silas Redd and wide receiver Justin Brown—the team's best offensive weapons—were looking sharp. Two virtual unknowns were turning heads: Zach Zwinak, a 226-pound redshirt sophomore recruited as a fullback but who was running like a tailback, and wide receiver Allen Robinson, a teammate of Bolden's at Orchard, a Michigan high school, who didn't play much as a true freshman in 2011, catching just three passes for 29 yards. Roof had tweaked but not changed the basic 4-3 defense, and the defensive line—with senior tackle Jordan Hill—and the linebacking corps that includes senior Gerald Hodges were the strengths of the team. But the style and scheme of the secondary was altered, and without any returning starters in the secondary, there was a lack of depth, and this appeared to be the team's biggest weakness in the fall.

Although the media is only allowed so see the last hour of practice each week, they are flabbergasted to find O'Brien's wife and youngest son on the sideline, along with the families of other coaches and staff. That was unheard of in the Paterno years. Paterno had a famous blue line painted at the practice field entrance to remind his players to concentrate only on football and nothing else when they crossed that line. If he had seen anyone's wife, including his own, near the field, except for an emergency, he would have chased them away with his high-pitched, squeaky voice.

Scott Radecic, a second-team All-American linebacker for Penn State's first national championship team in 1982, told me about that blue line a few years ago: "[Coach Paterno] said, 'When you cross that blue line, you forget about everything else in your life—your classes, your family, your girlfriend—for the next two hours, because you can't do anything about that. That's the time for you to focus on football. And when practice is over and you cross that blue line and you walk off the field, you forget about what happened at practice—a fumble or dropped pass or missed block or tackle. Forget about it, because there is nothing you can do about it. [That] is the time to focus on your classes, your tests, your girlfriend, your family.'"

Bill O'Brien believes in a similar philosophy, and you won't find any girlfriends, wives, or mothers of the players hanging around practice. He doesn't need a blue line to remind his players. His intensity, the sometimes harsh words emanating continually from his mouth, and the fast pace of his practices do that for him.

Saturday, April 21, 2012

An estimated 60,000 fans, the fourth-largest crowd since the Blue-White game began in 1951, turned out on an overcast day, with showers threatening, to watch Penn State's glorified intrasquad scrimmage. In a break with tradition when the squad was almost equally divided to form two teams, O'Brien instead matched the Lions defense (blue) against the offense (white) with a unique scoring system he devised with his coaches. The defense won 77–65 and scored 62 points on eight sacks and five interceptions—three of them by Rob Bolden, who completed just half of his 14 pass attempts for 78 yards.

Although little-used substitute senior quarterback Shane McGregor was the only one who played well, based on what the media and fans saw, Bolden was last in the quarterback derby, with McGloin barely in front of Jones. McGloin was 6-for-13 for 105 yards and a touchdown, with Jones 6-for-15 for 113 yards and a touchdown, but both threw an interception and were sacked twice. After the game, the coaches said they showed only 10 percent of the offense and 8 percent of the defense. The offense scored four touchdowns, one each by the young backup tailbacks, onetime fullback Zach Zwinak and receiver-turned–running back Bill Belton.

Many of the fans left after the first half and before the rain fell later in the second half. But they didn't need Penn State's beat reporters watching the entire game from the press box to tell them what they already had seen for themselves.

"What they did see [of the offense] Saturday afternoon did little to ease the fears about the team's quarterbacks," wrote Walt Moody, sports editor of the *Centre Daily Times.*

"None of the three battling for the starting job distinguished themselves," reported Scott Brown of the *Pittsburgh Review*, "leaving the quarterback picture as cloudy as the skies that loitered over Happy Valley before dumping rain on it late yesterday afternoon."

"Eventually, though, life is going to get real exciting for PSU's starting quarterback," wrote Bob Flounders of the *(Harrisburg) Patriot-News*, "because everything I've heard about the offense, the one O'Brien developed when he was offensive coordinator with the New England Patriots, is that it's all about the play of the quarterback.... O'Brien's offense is going to be balanced and it's designed to exploit mismatches. But soon after breaking the huddle, it's up to the QB to decide who goes where. The mental burden on the PSU QB will be huge. And that is a departure from past PSU offenses. The late Joe Paterno's QBs were, um, limited by the called play."

Blue-White games are fun for the fans because they are just another reason to tailgate with friends and to show the team they have a loyal following. Admission and parking are free. These intrasquad scrimmages concluding spring practice have become another college football tradition, and the attendance at this year's Penn State game was the third-highest of 28 BCS schools, just behind Big Ten archrival Ohio State's 81,112 and defending national champion Alabama's 78,526. In the last 10 years, thanks in part to the now-departed marketing mastermind Guido D'Elia, the event has turned into a three-day party with a carnival, rock bands, a wingfest contest, Friday night fireworks, a pregame autograph session with the players, and a Sunday morning Beaver Stadium 5K Run/Family Fun Walk at Beaver Stadium to benefit the Special Olympics. This game is now a far cry away from the initial Blue-White game in 1951, when an estimated 500 showed up on a cold and windy Saturday afternoon in May to watch the scrimmage at the State College High School football field.

In the past, the game has signaled the beginning of another upcoming football season but a long four-month wait before Penn State football is back in the limelight with the start of preseason practice in early August. Not this year. The Sandusky scandal has made sure of that, with his trial scheduled for June, a report due in the summer by Louis Freeh and his investigators, and the still-uncertain penalties promised by the NCAA. It is going to be a long, hot summer.

Monday, April 30 to Wednesday, May 16, 2012

What started out as a modest marketing strategy to have Penn State's new head coach, Bill O'Brien, and a couple other head coaches socialize with a few alumni chapters in Pennsylvania turned into a unique three-week, seven-day, 18-event blitz across six states and the District of Columbia. It was dubbed the Coaches Caravan, with O'Brien the headline speaker at every breakfast, lunch, and evening reception or dinner, with nine other head coaches alternating so that one to three of them joined O'Brien at each event.

Those head coaches ranged from longtime coaches Char Morett (field hockey), Russ Rose (women's volleyball), Beth Alford-Sullivan (men's and women's track and field / cross country), and Denise St. Pierre (women's golf) to the newest hires—Coquese Washington (women's basketball), Bob Warming (men's soccer), Patrick Chambers (men's basketball), Guy Gadowsky (men's hockey), and Josh Brandwene (women's hockey). They traveled in a plush blue-and-white bus, accompanied by other cars containing athletic officials and alumni personnel, and at each stop there were media there to interview the coaches and to cover the event. The itinerary sounded like a looping Greyhound bus route: Philadelphia; Drexel Hill; Baltimore; Washington, DC; Richmond;

Bill O'Brien poses with three other Penn State head coaches in front of the Coaches Caravan bus before their appearance in Baltimore on May 1. The coaches are (left to right) Beth Alford-Sullivan, men's and women's track and cross-country; O'Brien; Pat Chambers, men's basketball; and Denise St. Pierre, women's golf. Photo courtesy of Mark Selders, Penn State University Intercollegiate Athletic Archives

Harrisburg; Hazelton; Allentown; Woodbridge; NJ; New York City; Hartford; Scranton; Altoona; Pittsburgh; Youngstown; Cleveland, Erie; and Buffalo.

The caravan is a big hit, with a record 900 people at the Scranton event, drawing coverage at every stop and from some national media as well—*USA Today*, the *New York Times*, ESPN, and the Big Ten Network.

"[O'Brien] is a hit [at a Richmond breakfast], and he is in charge of a program where it seems all 165,182 dues-paying members of the alumni association, plus thousands of others, feel an ownership stake," reported Paul Wood for the *Richmond Times-Dispatch*.

"Meeting with alumni Wednesday at a hotel in central New Jersey," wrote *USA Today*'s Kelly Whiteside, "O'Brien received sustained applause when he mentioned Paterno and nods of approval when the group was told all that is sacrosanct in Happy Valley—the vanilla uniforms and namelesss jerseys—will remain so. A buzz of excitement filled the room when O'Brien mentioned a new game-day tradition: singing the alma mater with raised helmets after games."

Mark Viera of the *New York Times* wrote: "O'Brien compared the [caravan's] long trips…to what it would be like playing minor league baseball. But he said they had enabled him to pick the brains of the other Penn State coaches, learning more about the university and what it was like to work there."

The bonding with his fellow head coaches on the bus was as significant for O'Brien as the warm welcome he received by the alumni everywhere they went. They not only came to know each other better, but they shared their private thoughts about the vagaries of their jobs, the internal politics and nuances within the athletics department, and other such things that can help a new employee—even one with the most high-profile position in the university.

The new head football coach, the man with the most influence in the department and the school, is one of them now—around the same age, a little younger for some and a little older for a few—unlike his predecessor, an aging icon who they liked and respected but who was almost like a god. They, too, are feeling the repercussions of the Sandusky scandal and trying to help the athletes they coach move forward under this black cloud hovering over the university. Now they have a peer to lead the way.

Friday, June 1, 2012

Early in his Coaches Caravan tour, O'Brien began telling reporters he had "a pretty good idea" who his starting quarterback would be. In an impromptu session with media at the annual Coaches vs. Cancer Golf Tournament held by the men's basketball team, O'Brien said Matt McGloin would be that man, with Paul Jones at No. 2. O'Brien said he had informed the squad earlier that morning and that he would have a depth chart soon.

Guy Cipriano, the new beat reporter for the *Centre Daily Times*, was there and quoted O'Brien in his newspaper the next day: "[Matt] was the most consistent guy throughout the spring and has good command of the offense at this point. He' a tough kid, he's a competitive kid. He showed good leadership. I just felt like he's the No. 1 quarterback. I feel good about those two guys. They have decent command of the offense and they are competitive. They both have interesting qualities and we will see how they do in training camp. They won't get as many reps as they did in the spring." McGloin told Donnie Collins of the *Scranton Tribune*, "This is definitely exciting.... I always thought that I should be in this position. But at the same time, I know how hard I need to work to stay as the starter. I am going to work my butt off, play really well and see how this team responds."

Tuesday, June 5, 2012

The depth chart was released, and erstwhile two-year starter Bolden was listed at No. 3.

Unfortunately, the No. 3 quarterback (along with three scheduled offensive starters and a specialist) would no longer be on the team when preseason camp opened. The continued reverberations from the Sandusky scandal nearly destroyed the team as much of the national media cheered and Penn State's multitudes of fans cried foul. Eventually the leadership O'Brien had told the team he would need from them, on that first day of practice, emerged and turned a possible disastrous 2012 season into one Penn State will never forget.

But we didn't know any of that at the time…

Bolden's demotion is not really a surprise, but there are some. The depth chart has two tight end positions, just as O'Brien had at New England and with the same position terminology as the Patriots: an *H* slot and a *Y* slot. There are also three wide receivers, a tailback, and a fullback, boosting the starters to an impossible 13. At one wide receiver position sophomore Allen Robinson and redshirt junior Shawney Kersey are both listed as the possible starter. According to the news release accompanying the depth chart, the Lions will start preseason practice on August 6 with "35 letter winners and 10 starters for the upcoming season (5 offense, 4 defense, 1 specialist), as well as 17 players that have starting experience."

I am intrigued that three tight ends could be in a game at the same time as an integral part of a Penn State offense. In the past, the Penn State tight end almost seemed to be an afterthought and used mostly for blocking. I won't believe this until I see it.

Chapter 5

The Long, Hot Summer

Tuesday, June 5 to Friday, June 25, 2012

After a four-week trial at the Centre County Courthouse that again attracted another horde of national media and focused more negative attention on Penn State on June 22, 2012, Jerry Sandusky was convicted of 45 counts of child sex abuse involving 10 boys and locked up to await sentencing. The Penn State football players, who were working out at Lasch without the coaches—except for the strength training staff, per NCAA rules—did not follow the trial closely. But they couldn't avoid hearing or reading about it on television, radio, and the Internet, and even in the classes many were taking during the school's summer academic semester.

With Sandusky's conviction, a large faction of the national media and some within the state have begun angrily assailing the university and the State College–area community with renewed venom toward Joe Paterno and the Penn State football team. Some have called for the NCAA to immediately implement its so-called "death penalty" on Penn State football, which would shut down the program for one year or more.

"Jerry Sandusky deserves the death penalty. So does Penn State," wrote *Orlando Sentinel* columnist George Diaz on June 23. "This is the most despicable crime in the history of college football…. SMU got the death penalty because boosters threw cash money at players. That's a misdemeanor compared to this."

Kevin Sarbinsky of the *Birmingham News* agreed in his column of June 24: "Sandusky should get life in prison. Penn State could get the death penalty. If not them, who? If not now, when?"

The *(Nashville) Tennessean* columnist David Climer did not feel the NCAA had legal authority but favored the same sentiment in his column on June 25: "This should be a self-imposed penalty. Put the program on ice as acknowledgment that the university is guilty of allowing Jerry Sandusky's monstrous behavior to continue— often on campus. Penn State's leadership—assuming there really is leadership—needs to take a long, hard look at itself and do the right thing by going dark for a football season."

From what I have personally seen, read, and, heard in the media during and in these few days after the trial, the majority opinion is that Penn State officials—particularly Paterno, athletics director Tim Curley, and dismissed president Graham Spanier—have known about Sandusky's behavior since at least 1998 and did nothing about it.

The fact that the three men have not yet had the opportunity to defend themselves in a legal process does not seem to matter. They, and others associated with Penn State, are guilty, according to critics, and their alleged motive was to protect the football program. None of this has been proven and is pure speculation based on many assumptions and distorted interpretations of what actually happened.

However, all this is being completely ignored by a myopic segment of the media determined to condemn Penn State for eternity. The Penn State football team should pay dearly, they say, even if the current players are as innocent as Sandusky's unfortunate victims.

The black cloud over a community with the nickname of Happy Valley is going to be there for a long time. The headline of a posttrial analysis by Michael R. Sisak in the *(Wilkes-Barre) Citizens' Voice* on June 25 summed it up perfectly for me: MIDNIGHT IN THE VALLEY OF GOOD AND EVIL.

Thursday, July 12, 2012

No diary entry for this day, but it was certainly an important one.

At 9:00 AM Louis Freeh issued to the news media a 267-page document on his committee's nearly eight-month-long investigation of Penn State University's role in the Sandusky scandal, and an hour later he held a nationally televised 45-minute news conference at his Philadelphia office. The Penn State Board of Trustees, which paid at least $6.5 million for the investigation, was starting a two-day meeting at the university's branch campus in Wilkes-Barre. The trustees were given a copy of the report prior to its public release, but they did not meet personally or talk with Freeh about his findings before or after Freeh's news conference.

The report was explosive, damning, and severe, alleging a conspiracy by Paterno, Spanier, Curley, and Schultz to cover up Sandusky's child sex abuse since at least 1998. "Our most saddening and sobering finding is the total disregard for the safety and welfare of Sandusky's child victims by the most senior leaders at Penn State," Freeh said at his news conference. He went on to say that the motive for the cover-up was to protect the football team and the university from negative publicity and embarrassment that would have threatened football's annual financial windfall, which benefits the entire university. Freeh asserted that Paterno led a rogue football program that was out of control and "lived by its own rules" in what he termed a "Penn State culture" where the academic mission of the university was subservient to a football above all mentality. Freeh made 123 recommendations to rectify Penn State's problem, but he did not advocate a shutdown of the football program.

The details of the Freeh Report and the ensuing controversy that it ignited continue to this day. I believe the report is deeply flawed and fraudulent in parts, and other experts have agreed. However, this is not a book about the scandal. My only concern here is the impact and aftereffects the scandal and the Freeh Report had on the 2012 football team.

Friday, July 13, 2012

At the public meeting of the board of trustees today, the board informally accepted the Freeh Report but did not take a vote, nor was the report discussed in the open meeting. Chairwoman Karen Peetz said, "The board takes these recommendations seriously, and they will result in changes, beginning here and beginning today."

The football team's annual and prestigious Lift for Life charity event was overshadowed by the media and public's reaction to the Freeh Report. Lift for Life is an extreme but playful strength-training and exercise competition in which the players team up to carry out a series of challenges. With the public encouraged to attend, the two-hour-plus event raises money for the Kidney Cancer Association. It was created by former Penn State receiver Scott Shirley in 2003, shortly after his father was diagnosed with kidney cancer. It has been so successful at Penn State that Shirley has taken the concept nationwide.

As of the summer of 2013, there were 14 chapters on college campuses organized under the nonprofit organization's formal name, Uplifting Athletes Lift for Life, that benefit various rare diseases. Since the beginning of Penn

Penn State's starting quarterback Matt McGloin (center) leads the offense (on the left) to a victory over the defense in the exciting tug-of-war finale at the 10th annual Uplifting Athletes Lift for Life charity event that raises money to fight kidney cancer.
Photo courtesy of Mark Selders, Penn State University Intercollegiate Athletic Archives

State's event and the chapter's ancillary projects, more than $700,000 has been raised to fight kidney cancer. Penn State's Lift for Life is now held on the same weekend as the popular State College Arts Festival, which attracts exhibitors and patrons from around the nation.

But in 2012 the Freeh Report distracted attention from the Lift for Life, and it was on the minds of attendees and players alike.

"Anytime you turn on the TV or open the newspaper up, you see it," said McGloin, as reported by ESPN.com's Adam Rittenberg. "It is tough, but at the same time, you have to realize the outside stuff has no effect and doesn't control how you perform or the way you work. You definitely have an opinion on it, but I keep it within myself or just talk about it among my teammates."

Redshirt junior tight end Garry Gilliam told Jeff Rice of the website 247sports.com, "There's not much I can do about it. I wasn't involved in it, my teammates weren't involved in it, my coaches weren't involved in it…. A lot of my friends will message me on Facebook or text me and ask me how I'm doing, say they're thinking about me. We're focused on what we're doing. You can't control what's going on outside of our building."

If any media, including those in Pennsylvania, used any stories about Lift for Life, the item was more than likely buried in an avalanche of straight news stories, analysis, and commentary about the Freeh Report. Once again, there was another flurry of demands for an immediate suspension of the football program, and some of the criticism was scathing.

"I hope the NCAA gives Penn State the death penalty it most richly deserves," ESPN's Rick Reilly, one of the most respected sports columnists in the nation, posted on ESPN's popular website at 6:56 PM on July 13. He continued, "The worst scandal in college football history deserves the worst penalty the NCAA can give."

The next day Reilly's ESPN colleague, Howard Bryant, wrote, "Penn State cannot be allowed to have a football team."

In an editorial, the second-largest newspaper in the state, the *Pittsburgh Post-Gazette*, stated: "The [Freeh Report] evidence says football trumped everything at Penn State, when the university's mission really is to educate young people. For that reason Penn State should suspend its football program until the university has sufficiently regained its perspective and reset its priorities."

In the July 23 issue of *Sports Illustrated*, Michael Rosenberg wrote, "For decades Penn State football fans claimed their program was different, better and purer than others—a model for all college sports, but former FBI director Louis Freeh's 267-page report blew a hole through that claim last Thursday. It is withering, thorough, believable…"

There were some media defenders against shutting down the football team, sometimes from odd sources, including Democratic political advisor–turned–TV and radio commentator James Carville, who is an avid Louisiana State fan. "That is a really dumb idea," Carville said on ABC-TV's Sunday public affairs program *This Week*. "Lives have been ruined, so the answer to it, let's go out and ruin more lives? Let's take a kid who's a football player who was in the second grade when this happened and let's suspend the program. Who knows what he's going to do with his education? Let's take every contract that's been signed…everybody that has a motel in Happy Valley, let's ruin their lives as a retaliation."

David Zirin, sports editor of the liberal political and cultural magazine *The Nation* may have summed it up best in his weekly column posted on the magazine's website on July 15: "It's an act of collective punishment. The end of football at Penn State would also mean the end of football revenue underwriting the Penn State athletic department. It would mean the end of every athletic scholarship, every women's sports program and every one of the thousands and thousands of jobs produced by this regional economic engine. None of these people were responsible for Sandusky's reign of terror and Joe Paterno's [alleged] criminal complicity. The argument for collective punishment is always morally repugnant…"

Whether the Freeh Report was truly factual and accurate was rarely questioned by the media, and the Penn Staters who publicly pointed out its serious shortcomings were—and continue to be—savaged as supporters of child sex abuse and Paterno sycophants.

For the first time, this year's Lift for Life was held outdoors instead of inside the Holuba Hall field house. The event also featured a revised format devised by new strength coach Fitzgerald that included new exercises and divided the participants into offense and defense for scoring instead of 10 or more separate two-man teams. That brought out a record crowd of more than 2,500 on the new lacrosse field across from Holuba to get autographs from the players and cheer them as they ground and sweated their way through such unique and strenuous events like heaving 20-pound medicine balls behind their heads and over goal posts, pushing 6,400-pound vans across the field, and shuttling sandbags. When the day ended with a tug-of-war final, the offense was named winner of the day over the defense, 176–146, with another $100,000 headed for the Kidney Cancer Association.

Bill O'Brien, his coaches, and his players are trying not to be bothered by continuing pressure by the media to abolish Penn State football for a year or more. But they cannot escape it.

Monday, July 16, 2012

Paternoville, the popular student campout before home football games, became Nittanyville in an official name change by the student-run organization that oversees the encampment under the supervision of the university.

In announcing the name change, Nittanyville president Troy Weller said, "It's a new era of Nittany Lion football, and by changing the name to Nittanyville we want to return the focus to the overall team and the thousands of students who support it." Later, he told the *Daily Collegian* student newspaper the decision "was a culmination of factors" and "not related to the Freeh Report." Weller said the decision by the group's leaders was a "very, very difficult process" with "a lot of careful consideration." He said they informed the Paterno family through Joe's son, Jay, before announcing the name change, and that Jay "was extremely understanding."

What started as an effort by three students to get the best seats in the student section of Beaver Stadium six days before the 2005 Ohio

State game blossomed into a new tradition with a tent campout before every home game. On the Monday morning preceding that Ohio State game, three students put up small tents outside the student entrance at Gate A. That made them first in line to choose their seats once the gate opened.

In the past, students had rarely showed up at the gate until the early morning of game day, and occasionally a tent or two had gone up the night before. This time dozens of students started pitching their tents after the pioneers, and in a pattern that followed in numerical order after the first three. The original campers attached a large rectangular homemade sign that read "Paternoville" to the gate that first Monday afternoon, and throughout the rest of the week, before more than 75 tents were taken down early Saturday morning, a van loaded with Penn State football players brought the campers pizzas, a restaurateur well known for his barbecue ribs delivered 50 pounds of pork and bread, and ESPN several times reported live from the scene.

From the start, the Paternoville campouts gave the students another reason to party, but they were orderly, and alcohol was banned. The students showed up in rain, snow, and freezing weather until Paternoville was formally organized and rules were set up to ensure the safety of the campers, with temporary shutdowns in poor weather conditions. The tents have always been aligned on a first-come, first-served basis, which gives the students in line the first chance to choose their seats in the 20,000-seat student section. That means the early arrivals usually are the ones who sit in the first rows closest to the Penn State bench, where they are seen by the television audience.

Since Paternoville was first established in 2005, rules have been set up mandating the start of the campouts as no earlier than Wednesday night, except in special circumstances, and requiring someone to continuously man each tent. In case of severe weather, including freezing temperatures, Paternoville would close, and all tents would be removed.

Normally, the tents had to be dismantled and taken away by 7:00 AM on game day, and the students would stand by until the gates opened 90 minutes before kickoff. Joe Paterno would usually make at least one appearance each week to encourage the students, usually ending his visit by leading the campers in Penn State's famous cheer, "We Are...Penn State!"

I feel a special attachment to Paternoville. I was one of the first people to see Paternoville go up that first Monday in 2005 when I was running the Penn State All-Sports Museum. I had gone up to the second deck of the stadium to eat my lunch at a picnic table that almost overlooks Gate A on the east side of Beaver Stadium when I spotted the first tents. I hollered down to the students and chatted with them for a few minutes and wondered where it was going to lead. I was surprised when the three tents turned into a mini-village almost overnight. I also watched the tents go up for the remaining two home games, kibitzing with the early tenants as soon as I saw them.

I retired from the museum before the next football season, but whenever I am hosting new guests for a home game, I make sure we at least drive by what is now Nittanyville, and sometimes we stop so that my guests can get out of the car to take photos and chat with the campers.

Sunday, July 22, 2012

At approximately 6:20 AM, as the morning darkness slowly gave way to daylight, several workers, guarded by a line of 30 police officers, began setting up to remove the iconic statue of Joe Paterno along Porter Road on the east side of Beaver Stadium, near the student entrance gate. The bronze statue, installed in 2001, had become a major controversy since Paterno's firing, with supporters continuing to visit the site almost as if it were a sacred shrine and critics calling the statue a symbol of the child sex-abuse scandal that should be destroyed.

With the removal of the statue, the purge of the Paterno name was under way. One day later the pressure would intensify with the implementation of sanctions by the NCAA. Campaigns to name the stadium, the playing field, or the street on which the stadium is located after the deceased coach were either halted or slowed down. Some people even wanted to remove Paterno's name from the second library building that was constructed in 2000 after a major fund-raising campaign led by Paterno and his wife, Sue, who also donated several million dollars for the project. But more than a year later, Paterno's name remains on the library and also on his favorite ice cream, "Peachy Paterno," sold by the famous university creamery.

A small crowd of students and a few media members were watching from across the street as the statue came down today. Ben Jones of StateCollege.com had been sitting in his car all night, anticipating the statue would come down very early this morning. He was among the first to report what was happening virtually in real time, through StateCollege.com and Twitter. Using jackhammers, he reported, the workers began drilling at the base of the seven-foot, 900-pound statue at about 7:15 AM. Within another hour, they had strapped a blue tarp over it and lifted it onto a flatbed truck. A few minutes later, the work crew began dismantling the long concrete wall that stood behind the statue and marked some of Paterno's many accomplishments.

"The Paterno statue officially was removed at 8:20 AM, about 40 minutes after the drilling had started," Jones wrote. "It was taken inside Beaver Stadium for storage. More than 100 students watched the process and chanted, "We Are...Penn State," once the metal gate shut and the statue was out of sight."

Monday, July 23, 2012

In another nationally televised news conference—seemingly commonplace since the arrest of Sandusky—NCAA president Mark Emmert announced unprecedented and extremely severe sanctions against Penn State and its football team. Emmert said the NCAA's governing 21-person Executive Committee and 18-person Division I Board of Directors, composed of the presidents of various NCAA institutions, unanimously supported the sanctions based on the NCAA fundamental rule, "institutional control."

In a press release issued to reporters before the news conference, Emmert said the need for institutional control resulted from "an unprecedented failure of institutional integrity leading to a culture in which a football program was held in higher esteem than the values of the institution, the values of the NCAA, the values of higher education, and most disturbingly the values of human decency." Emmert adopted all the Freeh Report's allegations and claimed a "football first" culture took "precedence over the academic culture" and "led directly to the sexual abuse of children and the alleged cover-up."

This was the first time ever, in a major case, when the NCAA did not conduct its own investigation according to its own rules. Emmert claimed that was unnecessary because of the evidence presented in Sandusky's trial and because of Penn State's own independent investigation by Louis Freeh, which

Emmert asserted was not only thorough and comprehensive but was officially accepted by the Penn State Board of Trustees and the university president.

Emmert also told reporters Penn State agreed with the NCAA to "fast-track" the NCAA's penalties, signing the official "consent decree" that implemented the NCAA penalties and forever forewent any legal appeal of the sanctions. He admitted this was the first time the NCAA had acted in a criminal case as opposed to a nonacademic or competition rules violation, but Emmert said, "This is a very distinct and very unique circumstance."

Emmert listed the sanctions in the following order:

1. A "fine of $60 million on the university with the funds to be used to establish an endowment to support programs around the nation that serve the victims of child sexual abuse…. This amount is the equivalent of one year's gross revenue of the football team."

2. "Second, Penn State football will be banned from bowl games and any other post-season [sic] play for four years."

3. The "football team will have its initial scholarships reduced from 25 to 15 per year for a period of four years. In order to minimize the negative impact on student athletes, the NCAA will allow any entering or returning football student athletes to transfer and immediately compete at the transfer university provided he is otherwise eligible. Further, any football student athlete who wants to…remain at Penn State may retain his athletic grant and aid as long as he meets and maintains appropriate academic requirements regardless of whether he competes on the football team."

4. The "NCAA vacates all wins of the Penn State football team from 1998 to 2011 and the records will reflect these changes."

5. The "university athletic program will serve a five-year probationary period during which it must work with an academic integrity monitor of the association's choosing."

Emmert added that the NCAA reserved the right to investigate and discipline "individuals involved in this case after the conclusion of any criminal proceedings" and was "imposing other corrective actions to ensure that the intended cultural changes actually occur."

In talking about the sanctions, Emmert told reporters the "death penalty"—which had been handed out only five times in NCAA history and just once for football (against SMU for one year in 1987)—was considered and rejected by the two committees. "We had extensional discussions about the appropriateness of imposing a suspension of football for one or more years," Emmert said. "After much debate, however, we concluded that the sanctions needed to reflect our goals of driving cultural change as much as apply punitive actions. Suspension of the football program would bring with it significant unintended harm to many who had nothing to do with this case."

Almost immediately following the 35-minute NCAA news conference, Jim Delany, commissioner of the Big Ten, and Sally Mason, president of the University of Iowa and chairwoman of the league's council of chancellors and presidents, held a nationally televised 30-minute teleconference. Mason said the Big Ten had "legal counsel embedded with the Freeh group," adding that the president's council accepts the Freeh Report's findings and fully supports the NCAA action."

In answering reporters' questions, Delany admitted expelling Penn State from the Big Ten was part of "a range of discussions." He also said the conference "supports as much freedom of transfer flexibility as possible." Delany said the Big Ten could have banned Penn State football from all television appearances and the revenue-sharing from those games. That money would not be part of the penalty, and the Big Ten believed the additional loss of $13 million from bowl-game proceeds was enough punishment. Delany said the conference "has been damaged, but not mortally damaged," and Mason added, "This is not a proud moment for the Big Ten."

At the start of the annual Big Ten Media Days in Chicago three days later, Delany said the conference had been ready to enact its own strong sanctions if the NCAA had not moved beforehand. "You can debate [the sanctions] all you want," he said, "but in my view [the NCAA] had moral authority and responsibility to act, as did the Big Ten."

The NCAA sanctions drew overwhelming support from the media, with a bombardment of stories and commentaries that followed for weeks. Although there were some critics who argued that the NCAA overstepped its bounds and/or was too harsh, another segment complained that a multiple-year death penalty should have been ordered.

Even President Barack Obama weighed in during an August 3 interview with a Columbus, Ohio, radio station during a reelection campaign stop, and it made nationwide news. Asked by Mike Ricordati of 97.1 "the Fan" if "the punishment fit the crime," Obama replied, "I think it does. I have been a big admirer of Penn State football. Obviously, Joe Paterno was a great football coach. But there are some things that are just more important than sports, and making sure our kids are safe is more important than sports. And I think it was appropriate to send that message that we have bigger priorities here and we've got to make sure that we are always looking after our kids, and we have an affirmative responsibility to make sure that we're preventing predators from taking advantage of them."

One of the worst facets of the sanctions was the impugning of academics at Penn State (see my diary excerpt that follows for more).

Thirty former chairs of the university's faculty senate—including John Coyle, the now-retired longtime athletics department's faculty representative to the Eastern Collegiate Athletic Conference and the Big Ten, and John Nichols from the coaching search committee— also disputed the generalization about academics being subjugated by a "culture of football." In an extended public statement released on August, 28, the 30 past chairs wrote in part, "As a document in which evidence, facts, and logical argument are marshaled to support conclusions and recommendations, the Freeh Report fails badly…. The NCAA cites no document that proves their truth, as the Freeh Report certainly does not do so. Not only are these assertions about the Penn State culture unproven, but we declare them to be false." But the media virtually ignored this letter and accompanying statistical data. To them, Penn State was guilty. Period.

In 2004 Emmert's predecessor as president of the NCAA, the late Myles Brand, cited Penn State as the NCAA model for combining academics and athletics. At the end of an extensive two-day on-campus visit, during which he met with representatives from the administration, the athletics department, faculty, and student-athletes, Brand stated: "Penn State is the poster child for doing it right in college sports." This was five years after Sandusky had retired, and yet Freeh and Emmert alleged that a corrupt "culture of football" was responsible for supposedly turning a blind eye to and even covering up his crimes. Balderdash!

Writing about the sanctions, Mitch Albom, writer for the *Detroit Free Press* and also a best-selling author of nonsports books, may have best represented the majority position when he penned, "As penalties go, it felt like a guillotine. That was the idea…. The Penn State saga is so morally offensive that just speaking about it brings blood to the eyes."

A few hours after the NCAA news conference today, Coach Bill O'Brien and starting quarterback Matt McGloin issued statements in regard to the NCAA sanctions.

O'Brien said he will do everything in his power to comply with the sanctions and help the university move forward "to become a national leader in ethics, compliance, and operational excellence. I knew when I accepted the position that there would be tough times ahead. I was then and I remain convinced that our student athletes are the best in the country. I could not be more proud to lead this team and these courageous and humble young men into the upcoming 2012 season. Together we are committed to building a better athletic program and university."

McGloin said, "We, as student-athletes, are being punished for going to class, graduating, being involved in the community, and playing football. Even though these penalties are extremely harsh, I am a Nittany Lion and will remain one. I believe in the core values I have learned in this program. It is not Nittany Lion football. It is Nittany Lion family. I encourage all players, recruits, and supporters to stay committed to the greatest football program in America."

What angers me most about all the negative criticism of Paterno and the Penn State football team since Paterno's firing is the way much of the media—and the public it influences—has been jumping to conclusions while the judicial process is still under way and accepting as fact everything the Freeh Report and NCAA have claimed. Even a tiny bit of investigation would have uncovered major flaws and distortions in both reports.

As I wrote earlier, this is not the place to debate the merits of the Freeh Report, and I now add the NCAA sanctions to that statement. However, there is one particularly pivotal allegation by both that reflects—and will continue to reflect—negatively on the public's perception of the 2012 football team: that academics in Penn State football were a woeful second to a win-at-any-costs "culture of football." This was and is a gross falsehood, and the contention was challenged almost immediately with facts, including the football team's graduation rates taken from the NCAA's own records as well as from the US Department of Education.

For example, since 1996, the team's graduation percentage has hovered between the high 70s and low 80s, far exceeding that of most other Division I and I-A schools and public universities and on par with the graduation rates of Penn State's entire student body. In the 2011 season Graduation Success Rate (GSR) reported by the NCAA for football players enrolled from 2001 to 2004, Penn State's GSR of 87 percent was second to Northwestern in the Big Ten Conference and tied with Stanford for No. 10 overall among the country's 120 Football Bowl Subdivision (FBS) schools. And in a survey by the New American Foundation that compared NCAA and federal data on team graduation rates and academic progress rates of the 25 top teams in the final 2011 BCS rankings to the general student body, Penn State was ranked No. 1 with 117 points followed by Boise State (107), TCU (101), and Stanford (100).

Thanks to the media, the governor, the botched firing of Paterno by the university's own board of trustees, the Freeh Report, and the NCAA sanctions, what started out as "the Sandusky scandal" is now known around the world as "the Penn State scandal." At this juncture, July 23, 2012, outside of the abuse victims and their families, the Paternos, and the three officials still awaiting trial and their families, no one is being hurt more by Sandusky's crimes than the 100 members of the 2012 football team.

Chapter 6

Hell Week Plus One

Monday, July 23 to Monday, July 30, 2012

These were the worst eight days of the entire 2012 season for the Penn State football team, going back to the hiring of their new head coach in January and spanning all the way through the season to the end of the year. Almost from the moment Mark Emmert revealed the NCAA's draconian sanctions against Penn State, the players began receiving telephone calls, emails, and tweets from college football coaches across the nation. Sanction No. 3—allowing the 2012 players "to transfer and immediately compete at the transfer university"—meant it was open season for the fratricidal collegiate football coaching fraternity. Free agency, almost on par with the NFL except for the money, struck like a gigantic thunderbolt on a major college football team for the first time in history. It had become a serious game of every-man-for-himself for both the poaching college coaches and the besieged and bewildered Penn State players.

During the week, the scope of the transfer rule was clarified, and it was even worse than first believed. Players on the current roster could leave at any time during the 2012 season as long as they had not played in a game. After that, they could transfer without penalty up until the start of the 2013 preseason practice. The only stipulation for the preying coaches was that their school's compliance officer was required to officially notify Penn State's compliance officer about the players they were "recruiting."

Big Ten commissioner Delany, publicly admitting his displeasure with Penn State for besmirching the league's reputation, added to the chaos by declaring that players could transfer to another conference institution. At the annual Big Ten Media Days on Thursday, July 26, Delany defended the decision reached by him and the league's presidents, saying "I've been on the side of slightly more liberal interpretations of those because I think that players should have a little more flexibility than what they had under our rules."

Read on to see the day-by-day breakdown of this week.

Monday, July 23, 2012

Some coaches descended on State College. Others tried contacting players by phone, email, and social media, while also attempting to connect with the parents of players. A few players were receptive, but most were not. Several players, not happy with their current status on the depth chart or for other personal reasons, began to initiate contacts on their own. This was a hectic day, and the tension was escalating around the Lasch Building, where the players worked out on their own, and at players' nearby apartments.

Illinois took the most aggressive action, with its new head coach, Tim Beckman, sending eight coaches to Penn State to entice the players. Even USC, still under its own NCAA sanctions for major recruiting violations that had led to a similar one-year transfer rule, restricted scholarship allotment over three years, and a bowl-games ban in 2010 and 2011 got in on the figurative free-for-all and openly pursued the Lions' best offensive player, Silas Redd.

Tuesday, July 24, 2012

As the pursuit of transfers went into its second frenzied day, some coaches were hounding players around their apartments and at the Lasch Building, and several players began using Twitter to pledge their allegiance to Penn State. Others leaked the information to media beat reporters. The NCAA's odious transfer rule was taking a toll on the mental state of the players and starting to shatter O'Brien's "One Team" concept with reports that several players, including some starters, were talking to the predatory coaches about leaving.

Wednesday, July 25, 2012

Michael Mauti and Michael Zordich, the legacy players who had followed their fathers to play football for Joe Paterno, had had enough. They took the lead and organized a meeting of players who intended on staying. In an emotional, hastily called news conference at 9:20 AM at the Lasch Building locker-room entrance adjacent to the grass practice field, Mauti and Zordich, surrounded by some 30 teammates, told reporters that they and the others were staying at Penn State. They spoke without notes. There was fire in their eyes, and their faces and voices showed the strain and pressure they were under but also what was in their hearts.

"We take this as an opportunity to create our own legacy," said Mauti. "This program was not built by one man, and this program sure as hell is not going to get torn down by one man. This program was built on every alumni [sic], every single player that came before us—built on their backs. We're going to take that right now. This is our opportunity to do that."

Zordich said, "We want to let the nation know that we're proud of who we are. We're the true Penn Staters. We're going to stick together through this. We know it's not going to be easy, but we know what we're made of. We know that through this grind that there's going to be tough times ahead, but

Surrounded by 30 of their teammates at an impromptu early morning news conference on July 25, Michael Zordich and Michael Mauti defiantly tell reporters that the players are fed up with critics of Penn State football and they are strongly reaffirming their commitment to Penn State despite the unfair penalties from the NCAA. Photo courtesy of Tommy DiVito, Penn State University Intercollegiate Athletic Archives

we know what our coaches and the university are made of. We're ready and willing to fight and stick together to get through this thing to the end. We have an obligation to Penn State, and we have the ability to fight for not just a team, not just a program, but for an entire university and every man that wore the blue and white on the gridiron before us. We're going to embrace this opportunity, and we're going to make something very special happen in 2012."

About 90 minutes later, the players released a formal statement through the athletics communications office:

"This team is sticking together. We aren't going anywhere. And we could not be more proud to be Penn Staters now. We look at this as a great opportunity to have the ability to bring back not only a team but an entire university. This team has taken on more adversity than any team has faced in history, which is a testament to our commitment to our teams character, our fans, and our university. One man didn't build this program and one man sure as hell cannot tear it down. This program was built on the backs of the thousands of great men who put on the Penn State uniform. Today it is no different. No sanction or politician can tear this team apart. No one can take away what this university means to us. We will stick together and create our own legacy. Our loyalty lies only with our teammates, coaches, fans, and families. No one else. It's not going to be easy but we know that we have acquired the strength that we have overcome and we will embrace our anger and burn it as fuel this season. We can't wait for September 1 and to be back in Beaver Stadium and playing for Penn State in front of the best fans in the nation. We ask everyone to come out, show the support, wear your colors proudly, and show that adversity makes the Penn State nation tougher and stronger."

O'Brien had given Mauti and Zordich his approval for the news conference the night before. At the time of the news conference, O'Brien was at the ESPN studios in Bristol, Connecticut, where he was doing a series of interviews on the network's various television and radio programs. He flew back to State College later in the day and planned to fly to Chicago the next morning for the Big Ten's annual media days. However, there was a possibility that the three players scheduled to be with him might not be going. The media was informed that Silas Redd, John Urschel (a junior offensive tackle), and Jordan Hill might be pulled off the trip, but there was no explanation from Penn State officials.

One week later, USC coach Lane Kiffin told ESPN's Colin Coward that he and five other coaches went to Silas Redd's home in Norwalk, CT, on this Wednesday, July 25, and met for nearly four hours with Silas and his family in an all-court press to lure him west.

Just how Mauti and Zordich emerged as the prime leaders was told months later in articles by three beat reporters—Frank Bodani of the *York Daily Record and Sunday News,* Scott Brown of the *Pittsburgh Tribune-Review,* and Nate Bauer of *Blue White Illustrated.* Here is part of what they each wrote:

Frank Bodani, October 30, 2012:

"Angered and shocked by that [NCAA] Monday morning announcement in late July, Penn State players who had gathered together threw trash cans, stormed out of the room, or simply sat in quiet disbelief.

"Few could even talk about it, even after a quickly arranged team meeting.

"Meanwhile, Mauti and his senior teammates realized their purpose and charge into action.

"Guys such as Michael Zordich and Matt McGloin, Mike Farrell and Gerald Hodges, Jordan Hill and Stephon Morris. They quickly looked to everyone else on the team, questioned them, challenged them, led them.

"'We wanted them to get the feeling that we put so much into this, we have so much experience together,' Mauti says. 'Why go somewhere else and start over? We were not going to let this happen to a place like this—a place we had come to love and respect.'

"There was only so much they could do.

"And yet, in a sense, there was still everything.

"So Mauti and Zordich led the mission, spending evenings in new head coach Bill O'Brien's office talking over the future of the team, which meant strategizing on how to keep as much of its current roster intact [as possible].

"Publicly, their actions culminated in creating a video that proclaimed solidarity to the university and to their team. Mauti and Zordich, ringed by teammates, spoke. But so much of the work that week went on behind closed doors."

Scott Brown, January 5, 2013:

"The efforts of Mauti and his fellow seniors started the same day the NCAA slapped the program with sanctions.... That night, Mauti and running back Mike Zordich showed up unannounced at the on-campus apartment of defensive tackle Jordan Hill.

"'We need to keep this [expletive] together,' they told Hill after he opened the door.... The seniors pledged to stay together almost immediately after the sanctions were unveiled, and they took the lead in persuading underclassmen not to flee the program....

"Mauti and Zordich kept detailed notes on every player and where each stood as far as staying at Penn State or leaving. The two players would work out first thing in the morning and try to stay in front of the fluid transfer situation in the afternoon.

"Nights were spent in O'Brien's office, as Mauti and Zordich shared notes on what they were hearing with the head coach and strength coach Craig Fitzgerald. Mauti and Zordich outlined scenarios in which a player might leave and what player or players he might follow out of Penn State.

"'Going to bed at 3 or 4 at night and waking up at 6 in the morning and doing it all over again,' Zordich said of the days after the sanctions were announced. 'We had it all mapped out.'"

Nate Bauer, January 2013:

"It really started last November [2011] and the stuff we went through..." Mauti told Bauer. "Our whole foundation was just crumbling beneath our feet. Everything that we were taught for four years.... That was a great senior class and we had a lot of leadership from them, those guys really taught [our class] a lot...once July hit and the sanctions, that's when [Coach O'Brien] really found out who [our leaders were] and what kind of people we were, just because we had to be.... [We] made our statement because we knew we had the opportunity. We could see the positive side and what we could do, what this season would mean and the position we had, which was to bring it all together and bring the community together.... It was really hard to wrap your head around at first, but we really did see it back in July when we made that statement. I don't think we really understood the true power of what we did until now."

Today's players statement was certainly the most crucial moment for the players on the 2012 team and one of the most significant in the proud history of not only Penn State football but the university. In two minuscule hours, Mauti, Zordich, and their loyal teammates summed up the heritage of all Penn Staters going back to the creation of the university in 1855.

If Bill O'Brien hadn't realized who the true leaders of this team are, he has now.

The headline on Jeff Rice's column later today at 247.com succinctly zeroed in on the turning point of the 2012 season: LEADERSHIP FINALLY EMERGES. "[This team] is unlikely to make it to Sept. 1 entirely intact," Rice wrote. "But the ones who stay will have in Zordich and Mauti and several others the kind of leaders Penn State needs to rebuild its program and its culture, the kind that the university didn't have in positions of leadership when it needed them most."

Zordich has not been perceived by the public or the media as one of the team leaders. He has always been accessible to reporters, but the position he plays, fullback, is the least glamorous on the offense, outside of the offensive linemen. He started out as a linebacker, was redshirted as a freshman in 2007, played on the special teams in 2008, but moved to fullback in the middle of the 2009 season and shared the position with Joe Suhey in 2010 and 2011.

Zordich and Suhey, like Mauti, are legacy recruits. Zordich's father, also named Michael but with a different middle name, was a first-team All-American safety and cocaptain of the 1985 team that lost the national championship to Oklahoma in the Orange Bowl on New Year's night. Suhey's father, Matt, was a star running back on the Penn State team that also lost the national championship game, in January 1979 against Alabama in the Sugar Bowl. Matt went on to play on the Chicago Bears Super Bowl team of 1985, and the elder Zordich played 12 years in the NFL with the New York Jets, Phoenix Cardinals, and Philadelphia Eagles. After the NFL, Zordich became a businessman in his hometown of Youngstown, Ohio, and his son followed in his footsteps at Cardinal Mooney High School.

Young Michael has one other legacy tie to Penn State that none of the others have. His mother, Cindy, was a Penn State cheerleader, and her cheerleader uniform has been on display at the All-Sports Museum for years. So it is natural for Zordich and Mauti, who is one year behind him, to maintain a deep relationship at Penn State.

Thursday, July 26, 2012

The Big Ten's annual two-day gathering of the media before the official start of the preseason practices concentrated considerable attention on Penn State and the NCAA sanctions, especially the transfer rule. Mauti replaced Redd and joined Urschel and Hill as the Lions' player representatives. On the first day, Mauti took his lead from O'Brien, who defiantly told reporters, including Mark Brennan of FightOnState.com, "Penn State's taken a lot of punches the last six months. It's time to punch back."

Mauti said the transfer rules were so nebulous that the players were being harassed. "There's [sic] been coaches hounding our players [with] 10 to 12 calls per day," said Mauti, adding that he had been contacted by at least 40 schools. "[The coaches are] on our campus, outside our classrooms. Even some coaches from this conference. At this point in time, the fact that there's no rules—the door has been opened. You don't have to have ethics in this game. That's the game they created."

Asked if they were interested in Penn State transfers, most of the Big Ten coaches said they were not communicating with players but might pursue those who initiated the contact. Michigan's Brady Hoke and Northwestern's Pat Fitzgerald took the high road, saying they would not go near Penn State players, even if contacted first, but Purdue's Danny Hope and Illinois' first-year coach Tim Beckman admitted they were actively approaching players. Reporters were flabbergasted when Beckman admitted he sent eight assistants to State College, but he denied they were on campus as several Penn State players had tweeted, claiming instead that they worked out of various businesses in the town. "We went to two establishments outside campus and called some individuals, and if they wanted to come by, it was their opportunity to come by," Beckman said. "We're just following the rules of the NCAA."

When O'Brien was asked by the media if he talked to Beckman about his coaches being at Penn State, his face tightened and he replied with a blunt "No." He did not mention Beckman for the rest of his almost two-hour-long session with reporters packed six deep at the Hyatt Regency McCormick Place Hotel. But he did talk more about the transfer rule, saying he had nothing to say about Silas Redd and that no Penn State player had informed him they were transferring. At one point he joked that if other colleges were seeking his players, it must mean they were talented. O'Brien went on to talk about the other sanctions, the team's key players, and all the players' loyalty to the university and the team.

"What will be the key to have success on the field in these upcoming years with the restrictions?" a reporter asked.

"The key is, number one, to keep this 2012 team together, which right now it is together. And we've got to continue to communicate with our players, and that's what we're doing on a daily basis, minute to minute, we're communicating with these players. So that's number one. And then moving forward, you know…I've heard the talk that this is so bad [for Penn State football] and what are we going to do. I don't see it that way…I see it as an opportunity. I see it as a little bit of adversity that we need to overcome…. If people were inside the [football] building and understood what type of people we have and what they've gone through in the last couple days or six months, they wouldn't say anything about us being dead. We're alive. We'll be alive and kicking September 1."

During his session today O'Brien also talked about the sanction that will limit the roster to 65 scholarship players over four years from 75, with 15 scholarships per year instead of 25. This penalty has no immediate effect on the 2012 team. O'Brien touched on recruiting while talking to reporters but did not mention any prospects by name because of NCAA rules. Keeping the 2013 high school recruits who have already committed to Penn State—especially two blue-chip players, quarterback Christian Hackenberg and tight end Adam Breneman—is another priority in O'Brien's plan to achieve on-field success despite the burdensome sanctions. Along with the radioactive transfer rule, the recruiting will no doubt continue adding pressure on O'Brien and his coaching staff throughout the 2012 season.

Various reports claim that standout kicker and punter Anthony Fera, a redshirt junior from Cypress, Texas, has contacted the University of Texas about transferring. That makes him the second starter to contemplate leaving, joining Silas Redd. ESPN reports USC coach Lane Kiffin met Redd at his home in Connecticut for three hours, with a source saying, "It went really well" for Kiffin—not for O'Brien. This is just the middle of Hell Week.

Wednesday, July 25 and Thursday, July 26, 2012

The Nittany Nation fan base was stunned, and many were angered, when they learned Bill O'Brien was contemplating a change in Penn State's famous blue-and-white uniforms that included putting the names of players on the uniforms for the first time ever. This news hit the Nittany Nation like an earthquake, effectively wiping out 125 years of Penn State football history. Rich Scarcella of the *Reading Eagle* subtly broke the story on his newspaper's website at 7:10 PM on Wednesday.

Scarcella wrote about a one-hour teleconference call O'Brien had on July 24 with many parents of the 2012 players. Buried toward the end of his story, which was gleaned from an unnamed source in on the call, were these paragraphs: "O'Brien also told the parents that he has talked to Nike about changing Penn State's plain blue-and-white uniforms, a staple of the program for decades under former coach Joe Paterno. He also said he's looking to put names on the back of the jerseys. 'It might be easier said than done [for this season],' he [reportedly] said. 'I'm not sure we can get it done this year.'"

Scarcella's story created a buzz the next day at the Big Ten Media Day event in Chicago. Asked at his news conference about the report, O'Brien did not confirm it but admitted uniform changes were being discussed with the players: "There's a lot of discussions going on with our football team right now. We've got a group of young men there, like I said, that are sticking together. And there's changes that have taken place at Penn State over the last six months that are reflected already. [This is a] new era of Penn State football. And some of the changes people will have to wait and see until September...1st."

O'Brien's comments sparked a number of media stories over the next several days, many questioning the coach's wisdom in potentially adding the names on uniforms.

"O'Brien has begun talking about [uniform changes] as if it's a fait accompli," wrote Dave Jones the *(Harrisburg) Patriot-News*. "O'Brien even mentioned a blasphemous possibility: Player names on the back.... If he's advocating the uniform switch—and I'm not positive he is—O'Brien might be a little tone deaf about this.... I just wonder if he's misjudged and stepped into a realm where he shouldn't.... Until two days ago, I never heard O'Brien make anything but approving statements about the uniforms. He did it in his opening press conference in January and throughout his bus tour through the state in May. I can't imagine why he'd change his mind."

Donnie Collins of the *Scranton Tribune* had a different take: "Nobody is suggesting a change in look for their duds is going to help get the Nittany Lions out of the mess they're in. But a fresh, new look might be enough to convince a few prospects over the next few years that getting in on the ground floor of something fresh and new at Penn State is a good idea. For plenty of reasons, this was never something Penn State wanted to do in the past. Now, it might be something it has to do."

The media stories had fans in a tizzy. Many were angry about any change from the familiar plain blue and white. Others wondered if any change would follow the ostentatious and garish ugliness of Oregon, particularly since Nike was the supplier for Oregon as well as Penn State. Putting the names on the uniforms seemed to be sacrilegious to most longtime fans but popular with the younger generation, and the controversy raged on until the first game on September 1.

Friday, July 27, 2012

No major news emanated from the second day of the Big Ten Media Days. The pursuit of players by other schools had slowed down since the Monday morning statement made by the Mauti-Zordich group, and other players were are reaffirming their loyalty to Penn State.

The Paterno statue was taken out of the stadium and transported to an undisclosed location on July 27. As of midsummer 2013, the whereabouts of the statue are unknown. It reportedly has been moved to a location outside the State College area. There has been a strong public sentiment to have the statue returned and placed on display in the All-Sports Museum, which is located around the corner of the stadium at the southwest end. Because of my continued association with the museum, I am frequently asked, "Where is Joe's statue?" I have no idea, but I do hope that someday the statue will be restored to its previous site or placed in another prominent location.

Saturday, July 28, 2012
There were more rumors of additional player transfers circulating on this day.

Sophomore redshirt linebacker Mike Hull, listed on the depth chart as the backup to senior Gerald Hodges at outside linebacker, is "mulling" a transfer to Pitt, his high school athletics director, Guy Montecalvo, told the *Washington Observer Reporter* today. Montecalvo said the onetime Canon-McMillan star "has drawn the interest of a number of schools regarding a transfer from Penn State and is mulling his choices…. My phone rang off the hook earlier this week. Schools chose to use me as a conduit to reach out to Mike."

Junior linebacker Khairi Fortt spent today visiting the University of California. On the depth chart, Fortt and junior Glenn Carson are both listed as the possible starting middle linebacker.

If true, this is further bad news. The departures of these two players will not only hurt the 2012 team, but their coaches have said both Hull and Fortt have the potential to become outstanding linebackers in the long tradition of Linebacker U.

Sunday, July 29

Silas Redd was reportedly spending the weekend with the coaches and players at USC.

Kiffin confirmed Redd's visit on Colin Cowherd's program, *The Herd*, on Wednesday, August 1, gloating, "At that point, I'm sure he knew that he was coming to USC."

Monday, July 30, 2012

It was confirmed that Rob Bolden and Tim Buckley were leaving Penn State. Hell Week Plus One was over, but there were more player departures just ahead that would destroy three-fourths of the foundation of the 2012 offense. Even before it started, the 2012 season was looking to be more forgettable than believed just two and a half weeks prior.

Onetime starting quarterback Rob Bolden was removed from the team roster today, and redshirt freshman safety Tim Buckley, whose father went to Penn State, became the first player to officially transfer. Buckley, a former preferred walk-on from Raleigh, North Carolina, is going back home to play for North Carolina State. Listed in the depth chart as second-team free safety, his departure will affect an already depleted secondary in 2012.

Chapter 7

It's Us Against the World

Thursday, July 26, 2012

While the Big Ten Media Days were proceeding in Chicago, two former Penn State football players who cohost a two-hour Internet podcast, *The Goon Show*, every Thursday evening began promoting their idea to support the players with an early morning pep rally before the following Tuesday's conditioning drills.

The "Goon" is Keith Conlin, a starting tackle on the undefeated 1994 Big Ten champions and Rose Bowl–winning team. His partner is Tim Sweeney, president of the 1,000-plus-member Penn State Football Lettermen's Club. They called the event Rise and Rally and lined up the Nittany Bank and Old State Clothing to sponsor it and provide coffee and doughnuts. "These guys are under a lot of pressure," Conlin said. "Some of us started chatting on Facebook about how the community might show our support, and this idea came up. The message needs to be loud and soon that the Penn State community stands with our team." Conlin and Sweeney asked fans to be at the parking lot between the back entrance to the Lasch Building and the indoor facility Holuba Hall by 6:00 AM to greet the players as they arrived for their 7:00 AM workout with strength coach Pat Fitzgerald.

Hundreds of Penn State fans gather outside the Penn State football practice facility to greet the players in a unique early morning pep rally called Rise and Rally organized by two former players, Keith Conlin and Tim Sweeney. Conlin (left) and Sweeney are seen here describing the rally for their Internet podcast, The Goon Show. Photo courtesy of Steve Manuel

The day before the event, John Schaffer, producer of *The Goon Show*, said they hoped 500 to 1,000 fans would show up. "We expect a couple of thousand people," Penn State's campus police chief, Tyrone Parham, said.

The Rise and Rally announcement is receiving a lot of media coverage, including brief mentions on ESPN radio and TV and by the Associated Press.

Tuesday, July 31, 2012

Fans started streaming into the Lasch-Holuba parking lot as dawn was breaking. By 6:30 the crowd was overflowing the lot and backed up against the walls of Lasch, Holuba Hall, and the East Area Locker Room building across from both facilities. The Penn State Pep Band was there, along with some cheerleaders and the men's basketball team, led by their head coach Pat Chambers. So was Sue Paterno, Joe's wife, standing quietly off to the side. A couple of former football players were in the crowd, including Adam Taliaferro, once paralyzed in a 2000 game at Ohio State and now an attorney and newly elected member of the Penn State Board of Trustees. He later told FightOnState.com he drove all night from his home in New Jersey to be there.

The fans were cheering, yelling, and chanting "We Are…Penn State even before the first players arrived, and many of them were carrying signs supporting the team. One large white sign with blue lettering read: WE ARE… MORE THAN A CHEER…A CODE OF HONOR. More than a dozen signs of various sizes were posted in the windows of the Lasch Building, including three with quotes of inspiration from Thomas Paine, Winston Churchill, and Vince Lombardi. The Churchill sign read: WE ARE…STILL MASTERS OF OUR FATE. WE ARE…STILL CAPTAINS OF OUR SOULS. Another sign singled out the two players who took charge during the height of the bizarre transfer-rule bedlam. The sign spelled their names—Mauti and Zordich—vertically, with other words intertwined horizontally in the names:

Many	Ama**Z**ing
Alums & fans	Seni**O**r
Unite	Leade**R**s
To Roar	**D**efine
In Happy Valley	**I**ntegrity
	Courage &
	Honor

Conlin and Sweeney were sitting at a table around the corner from the weight-room entrance to Lasch, broadcasting the festivities live on another

Goon Show podcast. The temperature was perfect, rising from the mid-60s at 5:00 AM into the 70s by the time the workout officially began.

The rally went off beautifully (read the details in the diary excerpt that follows). In fact, Conlin and Sweeney could not believe how successful their Rise and Rally turned out. "My expectations were far exceeded because of the limited amount of time we had and the fact that it was on a Tuesday morning," Sweeney told the *Centre Daily Times*. "But in the same breath, I must say that it doesn't surprise me that Penn State would rally like this."

The players were amazed. "Kind of surreal and breathtaking," senior tight end Garry Gilliam told Scott Brown of the *Pittsburgh Tribune-Review*. "It was shocking," Matt McGloin said to Mark Brennan of FightOnState.com. "It was truly a great sight to see…. You're not going to go anywhere and find this type of support or this fan base."

Zordich may have summed it up best: "I knew there were going to be some [people], but I didn't know there was gonna be this many, especially at six in the morning. I came through that seeing everybody, and I'm like, 'These people are crazy.' At the same time, you've got to love it…. It shows you what Penn State's all about. It's not just in the locker room. It's through the whole campus and all through the state. It gets you ready for September 1 and the rest of the season."

There were two other notable occurrences on this day that would affect the 2012 team.

Silas Redd, who did not participate in the morning workout, issued a press release in mid-afternoon declaring he was transferring to USC. "Playing football at Penn State has been a dream of mine since I was seven years old, and I will be forever grateful that this dream became a reality," the statement read in part. "This is the reason that the decision I have made is so difficult for me…. My teammates, my coaches—past and present—and the staff have provided me with a tremendous amount of guidance and support since I arrived on campus, and I can't thank them enough for their time, their advice, and their friendship. We have weighed the pros and cons of staying at Penn State and leaving Penn State, attending USC and not attending USC, and I can honestly say that, ultimately, this decision is about so much more than football. I continue to have aspirations for my life, and as my family and I considered the bigger picture—both on and off the field—it became clearer to me that USC will be the best fit for my academic, athletic, and personal needs over the next two years."

Redd ran for 1,241 yards in 2011 and was selected second-team All–Big Ten. Most of the media was all but certain Redd's departure would severely cripple the Penn State offense. PENN STATE WILL MISS RB SILAS REDD, headlined a story written by veteran college sports columnist Tom Dienhart posted on the Big Ten Network's website. He wrote, "Without Redd, Penn State will turn to [little-used] seniors Curtis Dukes and Derek Day along with sophomore Bill Belton to run the ball."

The media consensus was that Redd was a good guy, always cooperative and open with the media and well liked by his teammates. "Redd was well-grounded…worked hard, treated people with respect and didn't gloat too much," wrote Ron Musselman of StateCollege.com. "He stood up for his teammates. He was a better-than-average interview…[and] Redd was the best player on the team—period."

The other event on July 31 occurred in the early evening, when some 400 Penn State lettermen from various parts of the country returned at the invitation of Coach O'Brien to meet with the team at Lasch in a private session closed to the media. Among the participants were broadcaster Todd Blackledge, quarterback of the Nittany Lions' first national championship team in 1982, Franco Harris, Greg Murphy, and Adam Taliaferro. Before the meeting, Blackledge told Tony Mancuso, who shoots video for the athletics department, "If you're part of Penn State football, you're part of a family. It's all the guys who are part of it before you and all the guys who are part of it after you. These are very difficult [and] trying times for our family, and I think it's very important that as many as can, be here to support Coach O'Brien and his coaching staff and this young and new group of Penn State football players and just rally behind them."

Except for a few innocuous comments, what was said in that meeting never was disclosed by the participants, or the media who might have been told, until Scott Brown of the *Pittsburgh Tribune Review* wrote about it on January 5, 2013. Brown reported that O'Brien told the lettermen, "The boat isn't sinking. It is rocking." However, it was a "galvanizing speech" by a virtually unknown former walk-on named Rick Slater that had the most momentous impact and crystallizing effect on the team and the outcome of the 2012 season.

"Rick Slater joined the team in the late 1990s, at age 28, after serving eight years in the military," Brown wrote. "After 9/11, he reenlisted, and by the time O'Brien had asked him to address the 2012 team, the Navy SEAL had served five tours of duty in Iraq and Afghanistan.

"Players sat at attention as Slater brought to life abstract values such as duty and honor. He talked to them about how his life depended on trust and knowing the guy next to him would fight for him."

Slater told the players about going on combat missions. He said the SEALs had a motto while on those missions: "Charlie Mike." "That is military shorthand for the initials C.M., which stand for 'Continue Mission,'" Brown wrote. He continued, "Then Slater took off the football belt he had worn at Penn State. He told the players that it had been on every continent and that he had worn it during every mission. That, he said, was how much Penn State football meant to him.

"'That was one of the more powerful moments of that speech,' Mauti recalled. Slater concluded by exhorting the players to 'Charlie Mike'—continue mission. The words made their way onto T-shirts as well as the wall of Penn State's weight room. Players would often bark the words in unison after they broke a team huddle. And 'Charlie Mike' is the reason Penn State didn't unravel after opening the season with back-to-back losses for the first time since 2001."

Mauti taped Slater's words inside his locker, where he would see them every day.

"[Those] two key words," Brown wrote, "offer the simplest explanation of why this senior class will go down as perhaps the most important in Penn State football history: 'Charlie Mike.'"

To the players, "Charlie Mike" meant even more to each of them than the "One Team" motto. "That was ours," Mauti told me after the Brown article was published. "We liked the 'One Team' motto and bought into it. But 'Charlie Mike' had more meaning to each one of us. We talked about it all the time, like when we broke our huddles during games, and guys would be screaming it at halftime."

"One Team" was the inspirational slogan that included everyone supporting the 2012 team through this season of multiple assaults on the very character of Penn State University and its football culture past and present. "Charlie Mike" was the players' battle cry.

As the players started arriving at today's rally, people created a path for them to walk into the Lasch Building players' entrance. The fans cheered and called out the names of players with shouts of encouragement, exchanging handshakes and high-fives with the players as they walked by. By that time the crowd was estimated to be between 3,000 and 4,000. Conlin and Sweeney told the audience they were overwhelmed by the response of the fans, particularly on such short notice. Most of the fans lived within a half hour's drive, but some have traveled a long distance just to be part of this historic rally. Thomas Bellingham and his three-year-old son, Reid, drove from Louisville, Kentucky. Sue and Matt Koch came from Cleveland with their 12-year-old son, Benjamin. Sue, a Titusville native who graduated from Penn State, told the *Centre Daily Times* she and her family were not season-ticket holders but tried to get back for one game a year. "Because we support the team doesn't mean we support a monster," she said.

The rally went on with fight songs and more cheers and chants while the players were inside Lasch, changing into their workout clothes. Part of the crowd was allowed inside the practice-field gate, and the players had to wade through them as they emerged from Lasch and went through the gate, walking in single file through the rest of the still-spirited, cheering throng to Holuba Hall.

Normally, Holuba is where conditioning drills are held in the summer, because of the heat. But because of the large crowd, conditioning had been moved to the practice field, but the fans didn't know it. As the players disappeared inside Holuba for stretching exercises, the practice gate was closed but the crowd lingered, still chanting and yelling before they began to drift away. With about 200 or so fans still there watching through the chain-link fence, the players emerged from the side entrance of Holuba, and Fitzgerald began putting them through his 40-minute routine. Suddenly the gate opened, and the remaining fans were invited inside to watch everything close up. When practice was over, the fans surround the players as they wound up the session with their usual chant, "One Team," and as the players slowly headed toward the locker-room entrance, the remaining fans broke into the traditional cheer of "We Are…Penn State," repeating it seven times to the delight of the players.

Today's rally was not overshadowed by the bad news that Silas Redd will definitely be transferring from Penn State. The reaction from the Penn State players seems mixed. Redd is well liked, and he appeared to be developing as the prime leader, along with Mauti and Zordich, until the onerous transfer sanction.

Stephon Morris, the senior starting cornerback, posted an immediate reaction to the news on Twitter: "Wish nothing but the best for Lil bro Si Redd. Not only a great promising future as a football player, but is also a class act in society."

But All–Big Ten linebacker Gerald Hodges is teed off at Redd and any others planning to leave, and his sentiments speak for many of his teammates. "If you're considering transferring, then obviously this isn't the place for you," Hodges told reporters after the morning workout. "Obviously you don't want to be here that bad. We're all one family, and that's what family does—family stays together through the hard times and through the good times."

Last item for today: The meeting between the old and the new Penn State players was probably even more crucial to team solidarity than the loyalty of the fans at this morning's pep rally. The Penn State football legacy being passed on from year to year since 1887 and 1888 made Penn State one of the nation's football elite in the 1910s, 1920s, late 1940s, and the five decades of the Paterno era. It means not only success but respect. Playing football for Penn State lasts four to five years. Being a member of the proud Penn State football family lasts a lifetime.

Wednesday, August 1, 2012

Late Wednesday night, ESPN reported that Penn State's leading wide receiver, Justin Brown, may transfer to Oklahoma. "I haven't made a decision yet.

I just don't know," Brown told Josh Moyer of ESPN's Recruiting Nation in a telephone conversation. Moyer also reported that Brown's high school coach in Wilmington, Delaware, had been contacted by at least three schools interested in Brown, including Oklahoma, Illinois, and Cincinnati. There was no comment from Penn State officials, but this made Brown the first senior to express interest in transferring.

This is not good news, and another surprise. Brown has been telling teammates and friends through Twitter that he is fully committed to the team. The fact that the enticement is coming from Oklahoma is worrisome, as the 2012 Sooners are already being tabbed by the national media as a serious contender for the national championship.

Thursday, August 2, 2012

With the opening of preseason practice two days away, the team was hit with another ominous transfer when redshirt junior Anthony Fera, the Lions' triple-threat field-goal kicker, punter, and kickoff man, announced he was enrolling at the University of Texas. Because Fera's transfer had been rumored, this was not a complete surprise, especially since he played high school football in his hometown of Cypress, Texas. In his statement, Fera said his main reason for leaving was the deteriorating health of his mother—who he called "the most important person in my life"—due to multiple sclerosis. While Fera said he would miss "the Penn State football family I have grown so fond of over the past three and a half years," he said, "I've been afforded the opportunity to give back to my family…. I love Penn State University, my teammates, my coaches—both present and past—along with all of the great fans who have supported me and my teammates over the years…. I will be giving my all to the Longhorns but will always be pulling for my friends and Nittany Lions family as well." He further pledged he would get his bachelor's degree from Penn

State as he had promised his mother and Coach Paterno, adding "I will always proudly say that I am a Penn State alum!"

Of all the eventual transfers, Fera's was the most understandable because of his family circumstance. If there was any criticism of Fera's departure from the media or the fans, it went unnoticed.

Fera was the first Penn State kicking specialist to be the starter for field goals, punts, and kickoffs since Chris Bahr in 1975. He was the leading scorer on the 2011 team, with 62 points to runner-up Silas Redd's 42 points, making 14-of-17 field-goal attempts and a perfect 20-of-20 extra points. His place-kicking made him a finalist for the Lou Groza Award as college football's best place-kicker, and with his average of 42 yards, established on 64 punts, he also was a candidate for the punting award named after Ray Guy. This leaves an unexpected void in the 2012 team, which will now have to depend on rarely used backups who also are on scholarship, sophomore Sam Ficken for place-kicking, and junior Alex Butterworth for punting.

The fact that Fera is promising to become an official member of the Penn State alumni warms the hearts of the fans, who seem ready to cheer for whatever success he has at Texas.

Saturday, August 4, 2012

Penn State's athletics communications office issued a 13-paragraph press release about the opening of preseason camp on Monday. The first sentence of the eighth paragraph included Justin Brown as one of three senior starters returning from 2011, along with quarterback Matt McGloin and center Matt Stankiewitch. Later that day, multiple media sources reported that Brown was definitely transferring to Oklahoma.

Sunday, August 5, 2012

The Penn State football team officially reported to the Lasch Building locker room in preparation for preseason practice, which would begin the next day. Justin Brown's name was removed from the roster. That made a total of 10 players who took advantage of the transfer rule, including seven lettermen: Brown, Redd, Fera, Bolden, Fortt, and junior tight end Kevin Haplea, who joined Florida State. None of the players were from Pennsylvania.

Brown said little to the Penn State beat reporters about his departure. However, in an August 16 interview with the Associated Press, he revealed that he would get his degree from Penn State at the end of December because of his lifetime bond with his Penn State teammates and his respect for all that Penn State had done for him. "I'll always have good memories. I think I'll always look back on it in a positive light," Brown said. "I'll always remember the bond I'll have with my teammates and what we went through. Just because I left it doesn't erase everything."

Although he would be taking classes at Oklahoma, the credits would transfer back to Penn State. He told the AP: "If a lot of courses weren't going to transfer, then I wouldn't be at OU. I was going to stick it out. I never wanted to think about transferring." But the allure of playing for a potential national championship— and bowl-bound team that would be more in the spotlight and unhindered by a scandal was too much for Brown to stay a part of the besieged Penn State football family.

Pennsylvania players obviously feel the most loyalty to their state university and its football tradition and to their teammates. Many have been Penn State football fans almost since their birth. The Penn State football family has been figuratively part of their own family for years, even decades. They are staying and fighting back— against the world, if necessary.

Brown's loss is another severe blow to the Penn State offense. He had been the second-leading receiver in 2011, just behind the graduated Derek Moye, with 35 receptions for 517 yards and two touchdowns, and everyone expected 2012 to be his breakout season. There is no one else left at wide receiver with his experience. Senior Devon Smith, a clutch receiver with 25 catches for 402 yards and two touchdowns, left the team on June 20 for personal reasons. That leaves redshirt junior Shawney Kersey (10 catches for 108 yards), sophomore Allen Robinson (11 catches for 29 yards), and sophomore redshirt Alex Kenny, a defensive back in 2011, penciled in as the starting wide receivers. Uh-oh!

Brown also was the team's leading punt returner in 2011, with 27 returns for 220 yards. Of the four other players who returned punts last year, none have more than five, and only one of those players is back: redshirt sophomore defensive end and letterman Brad Bars, whose six-yard return was a fluke.

Monday, August 6, 2012

At 6:15 AM the 2012 football team officially began preseason practice with a workout on the Lasch field. For the first time in memory, the media was invited to attend, if just for the last 20 to 30 minutes of the two-hour practice.

After this morning's practice, the stories that some of the media reported before noon on their newspapers' websites would have given Joe Paterno apoplexy, because he was an obstinate believer in closed practices—all day, all the time.

"The first preseason practice had its shaky moments," wrote Mark Wogenrich of the *Allentown Morning Call*, "and there was a noticeable lack of depth in some spots, particularly the secondary, where receivers covered other receivers during position drills."

In his first two sentences, Bob Flounders of the *(Harrisburg) Patriot-News* wrote: "[O'Brien's] quarterbacks threw interceptions, lots of them. His new top tailback, wearing No. 1, showed speed and quickness on a number of impressive runs."

The media reported that Belton is running as the first-team tailback, and some referenced McGloin's standing as the first time there has been a defined starting quarterback at the start of preseason practice since 2009. They also wrote that linebacker Mike Mauti wore a knee brace and that two starters, redshirt freshman offensive tackle Donovan Smith and senior strong safety Jake Fagnano, stayed on the sideline because of dehydration and hamstring ailments.

At the end of practice, the media huddled around O'Brien for an impromptu news conference, and this is some of what he said: "We've got a lot of good things going on here. Number one is, we've got to understand why we're in the position we're in, and we've got to understand our responsibility to the community, to children and to child abuse organizations. These kids understand that, and we're going to talk about that quite a bit, and we're going to show what we mean by that.

"People have talked to me a lot about the kids that have left, and that's fine, and I respect those guys; they made individual decisions. But I think we've got to start focusing on the kids that are here. We feel really good about the depth at most positions. I think in the secondary we're a little thin right now, just based on numbers, but those guys are out here competing, and I feel good about where we started today. We've just got to keep getting better every day.

"I'm very confident the guys that are here today are committed. It's day-to-day [because any player can still leave up until August 27], but I'm confident in these guys. They got up at 5:15 this morning, and they came out and practiced. It wasn't great. It wasn't all pretty, but there were some good plays out here, and we've just got to keep getting better. I feel good about our camaraderie. They're hardworking, good kids. They go to class, and I'm proud to be their head coach. It's a close team with a really strong senior class that cares about finishing their careers on a high note. Right now I feel very good about that."

There are now 28 practices left before the September 1 season opener against Ohio U.

Chapter 8

"The Times They Are A-Changin'"

Tuesday, August 7, 2012

An earthquake struck at the heart of the Nittany Nation. In a subtle yet anything-but-routine six-paragraph news release, Penn State announced that the last names of players would be worn on uniforms for the first time ever. The reason for this seismic change was buried in the fourth and fifth paragraphs, below the explanation for another uniform innovation for 2012—the addition of blue ribbons for home games to show support for victims of child abuse.

"Coach O'Brien says after speaking with some members of the team, they made the decision together to add names to the uniforms," the release stated. "Players indicated the names on their jerseys also mean they will hold each other accountable to uphold the traditions of Penn State football, both on and off the field. We want our fans to know and recognize these young men. They have stuck together during tough times, and I commend them for the leadership they have shown. Moving forward, I'm deeply committed to honoring Penn State's traditions, while building a bright future for our football program."

Most of the media continued to be supportive of the change. Frank Fitzpatrick of the *Philadelphia Inquirer* wrote one of the more perceptive analyses: "With Joe Paterno dead, his football program buried beneath NCAA sanctions, and Penn State's reputation on life support, the plain-vanilla uniforms that were such a powerful symbol of all three never had a chance.... The simple uniforms, so un-hip that they became cool, played an enormous role in creating the aura of Penn State football. The Nittany Lions program, its supporters liked to say, was much like those uniforms: simple and clean.... With a few strokes of a sewing machine, Penn State will symbolically break from its Jerry Sandusky–scarred past, honor victims of child sexual abuse, signal the start of a universitywide [sic] rebranding, and, not insignificantly, possibly reinvigorate a depressed market for its merchandise."

There's a quaint aspect to the names-on-uniforms matter that is still not widely known. Nike is the manufacturer and supplier for Penn State's uniforms, but because uniforms have to be ordered months in advance so they are ready

Karen Caldwell, wife of Spider Caldwell, the Penn State football equipment and facilities coordinator, sews the last name of quarterback Matt McGloin on his jersey. For the first time in history, Penn State players would have names on their jerseys, and Karen did all the sewing. Photo courtesy of Spider Caldwell

for the first game, the names are heat-pressed onto a cloth patch that has to be sewn on to each uniform. At other schools, this usually is done by a professional seamstress company. But all the Penn State names were stitched to the uniforms by one woman, Karen Caldwell, wife of the football team's longtime equipment manager, Spider Caldwell. Karen, a full-time schoolteacher, had been mending the team's uniforms during the season for the past 20 years, and she volunteered to add all the names herself. She had barely two weeks to complete the job.

"I'd go over to the table and pin it and make sure it was straight," Karen later told Stephen Pianovich of the *Daily Collegian.* "Then sometimes re-pin it because if cameras are going to be on these, I want to make sure they're straight, first time in history we're going to do this. My arms were shaking, my hands, just thinking, 'Oh my word, the history of this.' So I just started sewing some."

Spider said he was planning to have the names sewn on by a State College business. "But [Karen's] like, 'Bring a couple home, let me see what I can do at home,'" he told the *Collegian.* "I thought, That's going to be overwhelming.... She put them on and said 'I can do this, I can do this. I think we'll have enough time.' She really pounded it out. I was proud of her." As such, Karen Caldwell enjoys a special place in the 2012 season.

Although Penn State fans have been debating the pros and cons of names on uniforms for two weeks since Rich Scarcella of the Reading Eagle broke first word of it being discussed, this is a bombshell. This makes it official, intensifying the controversy among the loyal fans.

Thursday, August 9, 2012

This was Media Day at Beaver Stadium.

The regulars who cover Penn State have eagerly looked forward to this day, primarily because for the last few decades of the Paterno tenure, it has been their first opportunity since the end of the season to talk to the players and the assistant coaches. They were strictly off-limits by decree, except for a few rare occasions or prearranged special situations. O'Brien changed that earlier by making the coaches and most players, with the exception of incoming freshmen, available in person or by telephone at certain times. (Keeping freshmen away from the media is the standard policy at most high-profile football programs.)

O'Brien has been the most accessible of all—almost from the day he was hired—at formal and spontaneous news conferences not only on campus but also during his abundant public appearances elsewhere. As a result, he is frequently quoted in the media, and he often covers the same ground about such topics as team morale, the performances of individual players, coping with the NCAA sanctions, the continued effort to help the victims of child sex abuse, and the ongoing effort to help the university, its alumni, and the Centre County community recover from the scandal. Still, the head coach's news conference on Media Day usually makes news, and this one is no different.

Aside from the assessment of players and continuing comments about team leadership and the ongoing sanctions, O'Brien today disclosed the breaking of a home game-day tradition involving the famous blue buses. Since the 1960s school buses painted blue have taken the team to the Beaver Stadium locker-room entrance 90 minutes or so before kickoff. Over the years, fans began greeting the buses, and nowadays a large crowd is there as the players step off the buses, led by the starting quarterback and followed by the head coach. O'Brien is changing that tradition too. "We'll have game captains [this season]," O'Brien told the media today, "and those will be the guys that step off the bus with me…before the

Wisconsin game, then we'll name permanent captains." Asked if he would be the first man off the bus, he joked, "I don't know. I might be driving the bus."

A writer inquired how he has kept the team together in the last two weeks with the transfer penalty, and O'Brien replied, "There were a lot of team meetings. There were a lot of individual conversations that I had with individual players...the common phrases are unity, one team, sticking together, commitment, education, 108,000 [fans in Beaver Stadium], TV, a great weight room, chance to develop as a player."

He also praised the team leadership: "We have a really strong senior class. That's where it starts. You can't say enough about our seniors. Hodges, Mauti, Hill, Zordich, McGloin, Stankiewitch, Farrell.... Then we have a group of younger players, guys that aren't seniors, that I think are really good football players that are also part of that leadership group. Billy Belton, Adrian Amos— one senior I didn't mention in the secondary, Stephon Morris— and Malcolm Willis. But getting back to that younger group, you have those guys, Donovan Smith, Kyle Carter. You've got good freshman leaders that you can see already in our freshman class. So we've got leaders all the way through the football team, and I think that says a lot about those kids, and we're letting them lead. That's been good. So it's a strong senior class, but it trickles down throughout the team."

After all the team has been through, asked another reporter, "are you taking that 'us against the world' approach, a chip on your shoulder?" O'Brien replied, "Yeah, when we play football...we'll have a chip on our shoulder just like every football team should. But at the end of the day it's not us against the world. It's about Penn State, these kids caring about their education, and the fact that they have a chance to go out there and do something pretty special in a lot of different ways."

Following the news conference, the reporters and the camera crews went out onto the field, as usual, and interviewed whomever they wanted to—players, coaches, and even the equipment manger, Spider Caldwell—sometimes in media groups and often one-on-one. It's always been a bustling and, for the most part, pleasant atmosphere. I have been there many times. However, there was something about this one today that was different. Everyone seemed more relaxed with the media. The underlying tension that pervaded the event frequently in the last decade or so of the Paterno era was absent. Paterno ran a tight ship. That was his style. O'Brien is doing it too, but in a different manner and with a heavier burden than Joe ever encountered. Paterno was ultra-successful with his methods, but Penn State football is different now, and change is in the air.

After an hour or so, the players boarded the blue buses and went to Lasch for afternoon practice, and the media was invited to attend the last 30 minutes of the session. O'Brien is not only bonding with his players and the Penn State fans but also with the usually wary media.

As they left, some of the reporters noticed the words painted on an equipment box at the sideline. It was the 2012 team's fundamental motto but set with a hashtag, in the language of Twitter: #OneTeam.

There are now 25 practices left before the September 1 season opener against Ohio U.

Friday, August 10 to Friday, August 31, 2012
Preseason practice continued.

An insider's diary could be filled with daily notations about the happenings at practice, not just in the preseason but during the spring and fall too. Even if the diary entries only were on days when access was granted to the media, it would become cumbersome and filled with a lot of information that may seem important on one day but meaningless as days pass. What follows for the next three weeks are narrative and/or diary entries for only selected days when something different or meaningful occurred.

Monday, August 27, 2012

Classes began for Penn State's fall semester. Preseason camp technically ended, and the practice schedule became based on usual pre–game day preparations, with modifications to accommodate the players' academic schedules. Additional walk-ons (players without scholarships) were now permitted to practice with the team.

Tuesday, August 28, 2012

The first of the half-hour weekly, in-season Tuesday news conferences for Penn State's head football coach in the Beaver Stadium media room began at 12:30 PM.

Today's news conference was televised via satellite for media to see anywhere in the country, and some cable sports stations also aired the news conference live or in later rebroadcasts. The format of these news conferences has been in place for years. The head coach first takes questions over the telephone from beat reporters and others who, for various reasons, are not in State College. The team's senior beat reporter asks the first question, and the other reporters follow in order of seniority, with one question each. Any other media on the telephone line are then permitted one question. This usually lasts about 10 to 15 minutes. Then questions are open to reporters in the media room, in no specific order but in a procedure in which the reporters must raise their hands and have a portable microphone brought to them.

Some of the questions and answers today covered the same ground as O'Brien's Media Day news conference and his other meetings with reporters following selected practices. Although it is not the biggest news out of the session, O'Brien disclosed he is breaking another game-day tradition by having the players dress at the stadium instead of at the Lasch Building before riding over on the blue buses.

Since the construction of Beaver Stadium in 1960, the team has dressed at the football facility, first at the East Area Locker Room, and ridden buses to the stadium. At halftime they used a small, barren locker room with a concrete floor and benches underneath the west grandstands. In 1983 a new Beaver Stadium locker room was constructed behind the south end zone, along with a media room. The players still dressed at the practice facility before the game and took the buses to the stadium, but their regular clothes also were shipped to the stadium so that they never returned to the practice locker room after the game. Even after a new modern, up-to-date locker room was constructed at the stadium in 2000–01 as part of a multimillion-dollar expansion project that increased the seating capacity by 12,000, the players continued dressing at the Lasch locker room. However, they were not fully dressed. Although they were taped by the trainers at Lasch, their pads and helmets would be awaiting them at the stadium. O'Brien's change means that even the pregame taping will be done at the stadium.

"I'm not sure what they did in the past," O'Brien told reporters, and then outlined how the team will leave the hotel where they stay Friday night, pick up a fourth bus at Lasch, and then take the same route to the stadium locker-room tunnel entrance. "I'm not trying to say that that's not a big deal," O'Brien said. "I'm just trying to say that what is a big deal is how we play when the ball is kicked off."

Most of O'Brien's news conference was basically a last-minute status report before the uncertain 2012 season begins. Some highlights, for me:

—"I think we're going to have to do a great job of controlling our emotions, because it's going to be an emotional beginning to that game, cannot deny that."

—"Mike Mauti has worked extremely hard in his rehab, and he's worked extremely hard in training camp. He's been a fantastic leader for our football team. I just want Mike to go out there and really play well because he's like a lot of these seniors [who] I've developed a very close bond with."

—"Matt McGloin is our starter, and he's done a really good job of coming in here in training camp and improving [from] where he was from spring practice…. Paul Jones is still the No. 2 quarterback, but I will say that [true freshman] Steven Bench has come in and definitely closed the gap."

—"I feel good about the offense. I think we'll be a multiple-personnel offense. We'll be in different personnel groupings throughout the day. I feel good about Matt McGloin and his ability to run the operation…. These guys have really grasped what we're trying to do…I don't think it's a real intricate game plan. It's just a game plan where we want these guys to go out and be able to play fast, play at a good tempo, and try to find some balance…. We've got to do what's necessary to win the football game. So if we have to throw it 60 times, we're going to throw it 60 times. If we have to run it 60 times, we're going to run it 60 times. Whatever it takes to win the football game."

—"This offense has never had just one go-to receiver. It's more about throw to the guy that's open…. Allen Robinson has definitely had a really good camp, but there's a bunch of guys there that have played well, starting with Alex Kenney and Evan Lewis…Shawney Kersey…. We've got some other guys there that have played in the past in Christian Kuntz and Matt Zanellato and Brandon Moseby-Felder…. And then we've got freshmen that have come in and looked good in Geno [Eugene] Lewis and Trevor Williams…. It's not an easy offense to learn as a receiver…. I think these guys have made big strides, and I look forward to watching them play on Saturday."

—"I feel good about the secondary…. Just like everybody else, we've got to go out and play and play well. I think they've been very well coached by John Butler…. We've got some younger guys that have come in and really improved, and we think they can help us."

—"I would like to see more consistency [in our punting]…. It's gotten better over the last three, four practices. Alex Butterworth will be our punter…. Like I've said all along, we can always go for it, too, on fourth down."

—"I'm counting on [the 12 freshmen on the depth chart] to go out and contribute. These guys are good football players. They're instinctive players that understand what we're trying to do offensively, defensively, and [on] special teams…. If they play, we would expect them to contribute in a positive way."

—"[Ohio University] is an excellent football team. This is Coach [Frank] Solich's eighth year with the program, and this is probably his best football team.

"There is a lot of this [controversy surrounding the team] that is a little bit more than football, and I understand that. But as we head into this first game…. Saturday, it's about football…. It's our first game as a new staff in basically a new era of Penn State football, so I just want us to go out there and do the best we can, work extremely hard, and play smart football."

Wednesday, August 29, 2012

This was the start-up day of the season for two pre–game day traditions—the weekly Wednesday Quarterback Club luncheon for the fans and the first campout at Nittanyville.

The Quarterback Club luncheon dates back to 1941 and features the head football coach and two of his players. It started with a half dozen or so State College businessmen meeting informally with the head coach in the backroom of a State College restaurant where the coach, originally Bob Higgins, would show film of the previous week's game. Nowadays, nearly 400 men and women, some of whom drive in every week from as far away as Erie, Williamsport, Lewisburg, and Altoona, gather in the Mount Nittany Lounge in the south end of Beaver Stadium. The only rule for the affair, which lasts from 11:00 AM to 12:45 PM, is that everything said in the room by the players and coaches is all off the record. With Paterno's illness in recent years, he made fewer appearances—just one in the 2011 season, October 12 before the Purdue game—and assistant coaches substituted for him.

As is customary, the head coach didn't show up until the player interviews were conducted by Steve Jones, the veteran sportscaster for Penn State football and basketball. Paterno always wore a coat and tie. Bill O'Brien arrived in his now-customary warm-up attire, but without a ball cap on his head, as Mauti and Zordich were being interviewed. He received a standing ovation before his question-and-answer session started and another heavy applause when he finished. O'Brien has just won over some of Penn State's toughest but most loyal older fans—at least for the time being.

Several hours later and four floors down from the Mount Nittany Club and slightly to the east, students began pitching their tents at the renamed campout, Nittanyville, outside Gate A, now lit up in the darkness. Nittanyville president Troy Weller told Mike Dawson of the *Centre Daily Times* he expects at least two dozen tents. "I think people are just ready to get back in Beaver Stadium," Weller said, "and do what they've been doing the past couple of years—just being loud and supporting these guys,"

Thursday, August 30, 2012

Another tradition debuted for the season—the head coach's popular radio call-in show which airs every Thursday evening from 6:05 to 7:00 PM. There was a major change in the format in 2012, though. Since the program began with Joe Paterno and host Fran Fisher, it had been conducted from a room at the football building. For the first time, the show would be conducted before a live audience at a local sports bar and restaurant, Damon's Grill. This year's program, now formally known as the *Penn State Football Show*, is being aired by a 50-station syndicated network that includes stations in New York, New Jersey, Maryland, and Delaware as well as Pennsylvania.

The live format became even more popular with Penn State students, thanks to the personality and enthusiasm of Bill O'Brien. Nittanyville campers jammed the sports bar's big main room and received assistance from O'Brien when he sent the blue buses to the stadium to transport as many tenters as could leave to and from the restaurant. O'Brien added another perk by buying his enthusiastic student audience pizza for dinner.

"The Times They Are A-Changin'."

Friday, August 31, 2012

A record crowd estimated at 21,000 turned out at Beaver Stadium for the ninth annual Football Eve pep rally featuring O'Brien and the football team.

This year there was a new twist to the Football Eve rally, which started at 7:00 PM around the goal posts in the south end of the stadium: 12 other head coaches of Penn State's men's and women's athletic teams were part of the rally. The Blue Band, cheerleaders, the Nittany Lions mascot, the Lionettes dance team, and a new football video on the Jumbotron pumped up the crowd before the team's arrival, and men's basketball coach Pat Chambers introduced a new chant—"O…B! O…B! O…B!"—that he said was for "our fearless leader, Bill O'Brien, baby!"

The fans cheered the loudest when the team walked in, and then O'Brien took the microphone in front of the temporary bleachers where his players were sitting. O'Brien said, "This is a very special group of players, led by a very special senior class that has made a commitment to this university, to this athletic department, and for this football program. And everything you scream for tomorrow, you're cheering for this team right here. Because this team can't wait to play tomorrow."

Kickoff for the 2012 season is less than 17 hours away.

Saturday, September 1, 2012

The Penn State beat reporters had come to respect and even admire the players for what they had gone through, especially in the preceding two months. But even before the sanctions hit, the media following the team had been predicting a consensus 8–4 season, 9–3 at best.

Two polls taken months apart—after spring practice and the beginning of preseason drills—aptly demonstrated the influence of the sanctions. In the late spring survey of 15 writers for the *Town and Gown 2012 Football Annual* magazine, seven writers predicted an 8–4 season and four chose 9–3, with another four picking 7–5. A poll of 20 reporters conducted by the *Altoona Mirror* on preseason media day had 11 predicting 7–5, five forecasting 6–6, and four selecting 8–4.

Depth Chart Comparison:
End of Spring Practice (June 5) vs. First Game (September 1)

2012 Penn State Depth Chart as of June 5

*= Fifth-year senior
†=No longer with the team on September 1

OFFENSE

Wide Receiver

8 Allen Robinson (6'3", 199, So/So) OR
81 Shawney Kersey (6'1", 199, Sr/Jr)
80 Matt Zanellato (6'3", 195, So/Fr)
85 Brandon Moseby-Felder (6'2", 188, Sr/Jr)

Left Tackle

76 Donovan Smith (6'5", 310, So/Fr)
70 Nate Cadogan (6'5", 283, Sr/Jr)
52 Luke Graham (6'4", 273, Jr/So)

Left Guard

65 Miles Dieffenbach (6'3", 286, Jr/So) OR
73 Marc Arcidiacono (6'4", 283, Sr/Jr)
66 Angelo Mangiro (6'3", 287, So/Fr)

Center

54 Matt Stankiewitch (6'3", 295, Sr/Sr)*
60 Ty Howle (6'0", 298, Gr/Jr)
66 Angelo Mangiro (6'3", 287, So/Fr) OR
62 Frank Figueroa (6'3", 303, Sr/Jr)

Right Guard
64 John Urschel (6'3", 287, Gr/Jr)
75 Eric Shrive (6'6", 312, Sr/Jr)
56 Anthony Alosi (6'4", 292, So/Fr)

Right Tackle
58 Adam Gress (6'6", 306, Sr/Jr)
78 Mike Farrell (6'6", 276, Sr/Sr)*
56 Anthony Alosi (6'4", 292, So/Fr)

Tight End—Y
89 Garry Gilliam (6'6", 277, Sr/Jr)
18 Jesse James (6'7", 265, Fr/Fr)
82 Matt Lehman (6'7", 247, Sr/Jr)

Tight End—F
87 Kyle Carter (6'3", 241, So/Fr)
10 Kevin Haplea (6'4", 248, Jr/Jr) †
32 Dakota Royer (6'1", 223, Jr/So) OR
82 Brian Irvin (6'3", 241, Sr/Sr)*

Quarterback
11 Matt McGloin (6'1", 199, Gr/Sr)*
7 Paul Jones (6'3", 245, Jr/So)
1 Rob Bolden (6'3", 214, Jr/Jr) †
2 Shane McGregor (6'1", 200, Sr/Sr)

Tailback
25 Silas Redd (5'10", 200, Jr/Jr) †
5 Bill Belton (5'10", 196, So/So)
24 Derek Day (5'9", 195, Sr/Sr)
40 Zach Zwinak (6'1", 226, Jr/So)

Fullback
9 Michael Zordich (6'1", 242, Sr/Sr)

Wide Receiver
3 Devon Smith (5'7", 147, Sr/Sr) †
15 Alex Kenney (6'0", 193, Jr/So)

Wide Receiver
19 Justin Brown (6'3", 209, Sr/Sr) †
81 Shawney Kersey (6'1", 199, Sr/Jr)
17 Christian Kuntz (6'4", 222, Sr/Jr)

DEFENSE

Left End
90 Sean Stanley (6'1", 247, Sr/Sr)
86 C.J. Olaniyan (6'3", 250, Jr/So) OR
31 Brad Bars (6'3", 237, Jr/So)

Left Tackle
47 Jordan Hill (6'1", 298, Sr/Sr)
84 Kyle Baublitz (6'5", 270, Jr/So)

Right Tackle
91 DaQuan Jones (6'3", 317, Jr/Jr)
93 James Terry (6'3", 317, Sr/Sr)*

Right End
59 Pete Massaro (6'4", 263, Gr/Sr)*
18 Deion Barnes (6'4", 248, So/Fr) OR
98 Anthony Zettel (6'5", 255, So/Fr)

Outside Linebacker
6 Gerald Hodges (6'2", 233,Sr/Sr)
43 Mike Hull (6'0", 213, Jr/So)

Middle Linebacker
40 Glenn Carson (6'3", 238, Jr/Jr) OR
11 Khairi Fortt (6'2", 238, Jr/Jr) †
33 Michael Yancich (6'2", 240, Sr/Sr)*

Outside Linebacker
42 Michael Mauti (6'2", 239, Gr/Sr)*
38 Ben Kline (6'2", 224, So/Fr)

Left Cornerback
12 Stephon Morris (5'8", 188, Sr/Sr)
39 Jesse Della Valle (6'1", 187, Jr/So)

Strong Safety
27 Jake Fagnano (6'0", 201, Sr/Sr)*
7 Stephen Obeng'Agyapong (5'10", 201, Sr/Jr)

Free Safety
10 Malcolm Willis (5'11", 205,Sr/Jr)
13 Tim Buckley (6'0", 202, So/Fr)

Right Cornerback
4 Adrian Amos (6'0", 209, So/So) OR
1 Derrick Thomas (6'0",181, Sr/Jr) †

SPECIAL TEAMS

Punter
30 Anthony Fera (6'2", 220, Sr/Jr) †

Kicker
30 Anthony Fera (6'2", 220, Sr/Jr) †
97 Sam Ficken (6'3", 180, So/So)

Holder
11 Matt McGloin (6'1", 199, Gr/Sr)*
4 Evan Lewis (5'10", 173, Gr/Sr)

Kick Snapper
60 Ty Howle (6'0", 298, Gr/Jr)
57 Emery Etter (6'1", 223, Sr/Jr)

Kickoff Returners
4 Adrian Amos (6'0", 209, So/So)
5 Bill Belton (5'10", 196, So/So)
3 Devon Smith (5'7", 147, Sr/Sr) †

Punt Returners
19 Justin Brown (6'3", 209, Sr/Sr) †
5 Bill Belton (5'10", 196, So/So)

2012 Penn State Depth Chart as of August 27

* Fifth-year senior
♦ =New starters since end of spring practice (June 1)

OFFENSE

Center
54 Matt Stankiewitch (6'3", 301, Sr/Sr)*
66 Angelo Mangiro (6'3", 291, So/Fr)
55 Wendy Laurent (6'2", 278, Fr/Fr)

Right Guard
64 John Urschel (6'3", 307, Gr/Jr)
75 Eric Shrive (6'6", 305, Sr/Jr)
62 Frank Figueroa (6'3", 208, Sr/Jr)

Right Tackle
78 Mike Farrell (6'6", 306, Sr/Sr)* ♦ OR
58 Adam Gress (6'6", 311, Sr/Jr)
79 Kevin Blanchard (6'7", 311, So/Fr)

Left Guard
65 Miles Dieffenbach (6'3", 300, Jr/So)
66 Angelo Mangiro (6'3", 291, So/Fr)
56 Anthony Alosi (6'4", 287, So/Fr)

Left Tackle
76 Donovan Smith (6'5", 316, So/Fr)
70 Nate Cadogan (6'5", 293, Sr/Jr)

Quarterback
11 Matt McGloin (6'1", 201, Gr/Sr)*
7 Paul Jones (6'3", 258, Jr/So) OR
12 Steven Bench (6'2", 204, Fr/Fr)
2 Shane McGregor (6'1", 211, Sr/Sr)

Running Back
1 Bill Belton (5'10", 202, So/So) ♦
24 Derek Day (5'9", 193, Sr/Sr)
22 Akeel Lynch (6'0", 209, Fr/Fr) OR
40 Zach Zwinak (6'1", 232, Jr/So) OR
26 Curtis Dukes (6'1", 245, Sr/Jr)

Fullback
9 Michael Zordich (6'1", 236, Gr/Sr)*
35 Pat Zerbe (6'1", 236, Sr/Jr)

Tight End —Y
89 Garry Gilliam (6'6", 262, Sr/Jr)
18 Jesse James (6'7", 264, Fr/Fr)

Tight End—F
87 Kyle Carter (6'3", 247, So/Fr)
82 Brian Irvin (6'3", 242, Sr/Sr)
83 Brent Wilkerson (6'3", 239, Fr/Fr)

Tight End—Y/F
84 Matt Lehman (6'6", 258, Sr/Jr) ◆

Wide Receiver
8 Allen Robinson (6'3", 201, So/So)
16 Eugene Lewis (6'1", 199, Fr/Fr) OR
80 Matt Zanellato (6'3", 198, So/Fr)

Wide Receiver
81 Shawney Kersey (6'1", 197, Sr/Jr) OR
10 Trevor Williams (6'1", 186, Fr/Fr)
17 Christian Kuntz (6'4", 218, Sr/Jr) OR
85 Brandon Moseby-Felder (6'2", 195, Sr/Jr)

Wide Receiver
15 Alex Kenney (6'0", 192, Jr/So) ◆ OR
4 Evan Lewis (5'10", 174, Gr/Sr)*
20 Malik Golden (6'1", 182, Fr/Fr) OR
88 Jonathan Warner (6'1", 198, Fr/Fr)

DEFENSE

Defensive End
18 Deion Barnes (6'4", 246, So/Fr) ◆ OR
59 Pete Massaro (6'4", 256, Gr/Sr)* ◆
98 Anthony Zettel (6'5", 253, So/Fr)

Defensive Tackle
91 DaQuan Jones (6'3", 324, Jr/Jr) OR
93 James Terry (6'3", 316, Gr/Sr)*
99 Austin Johnson (6'4", 297, Fr/Fr)

Defensive Tackle
47 Jordan Hill (6'1", 292, Sr/Sr)
84 Kyle Baublitz (6'5", 287, Jr/So)

Defensive End
90 Sean Stanley (6'1", 243, Sr/Sr)
86 C.J. Olaniyan (6'3", 248, Jr/So)

Outside Linebacker
42 Michael Mauti (6'2", 232, Gr/Sr)*
38 Ben Kline (6'2", 224, So/Fr)

Middle Linebacker
40 Glenn Carson (6'3", 235, Jr/Jr)
33 Michael Yancich (6'2", 233, Gr/Sr) OR
5 Nyeem Wartman (6'1", 236, Fr/Fr)

Outside Linebacker
6 Gerald Hodges (6'2", 237,Sr/Sr)
43 Mike Hull (6'0", 228, Jr/So)

Cornerback
4 Adrian Amos (6'0", 205, So/So)
39 Jesse Della Valle (6'1", 190, Jr/So)
1 Jordan Lucas (6'0", 188, Fr/Fr)

Safety
10 Malcolm Willis (5'11", 209,Sr/Jr)
23 Ryan Keiser (6'1", 200, Jr/So)

Safety
7 Stephen Obeng-Agyapong (5'10", 207, Sr/Jr) OR
27 Jake Fagnano (6'0", 206, Sr/Sr)

Cornerback
12 Stephon Morris (5'8", 186, Sr/Sr)
3 DaQuan Davis (5'10", 161, Fr/Fr)

SPECIAL TEAMS
Punter
45 Alex Butterworth (5'10", 206, Jr/Jr)

Kicker
97 Sam Ficken (6'3", 172, So/So) ◆

Holder
4 Evan Lewis (5'1", 174, Gr/Sr)* ◆

Kick Snapper
57 Emery Etter (6'1", 221, Sr/Jr) ◆

Kick Returners
TBA◆

Chapter 9

A Kick In the Butt

Saturday, September 1, 2012

Hundreds of screaming, cheering fans greeted the four blue buses carrying the Penn State football team as they pulled up to the locker-room tunnel entrance at approximately 10:30 AM. Men, women, and children were dozens deep behind roped-off lines, and some of them had been waiting for at least an hour. The regulars who have been part of this traditional welcome for years said this was by far the largest and the loudest crowd they had ever seen. When Coach Bill O'Brien stepped off the first blue bus, followed by his four senior game captains—Derrick Day, Jordan Hill, Gerald Hodges, and Matt McGloin—the cheering could be heard far into the tailgate lots.

It was a warm but cloudy morning today. By game time the temperature was 79 degrees and soared into the low 90s during the afternoon. The tailgate lots began filling up early, and the fans were in a festive mood. They have been waiting for this day since the last home game in mid-November 2011 against Nebraska. The mood was somber then, but this one was radically different.

117

Sandusky's crimes, his victims, the sanctions, and Joe Paterno were still on fans' minds, and they occasionally talked about it with their tailgating friends. But as their new coach has said, today was all about football, no matter what the nastiest critics think about Penn State.

Much of the tailgate talk was about the opening day opponent. Ohio U almost won the Mid-American Conference title last season, and with a veteran team, they are expected to win it all this year. Still, before the sanctions hit, Penn State was a heavy 17-point favorite. But that was down to six points by today.

Tailgaters turned their heads as the 310-piece Blue Band marched from its facility a quarter mile away, down University Drive, and into the Bryce Jordan Center for its traditional pregame concert. A half hour or so later, the band formed up again along Curtin Road and marched to the locker-room tunnel entrance.

By the time the band makes its traditional entrance through the tunnel and onto the field, most of the fans are already in their Beaver Stadium seats. They want to cheer when the Nittany Lions mascot runs to the middle of the field and lifts his upper arm toward each grandstand area—west, north, east, south—to see which section of fans can holler the loudest, and then all together. They want to watch the drum major follow with his run to midfield for his traditional somersault flip and then run back to the goal posts and repeat it as the rest of the band strides downfield.

The band went through its traditional pregame songs today, but something was added on this special opening day. Some 600 athletes from Penn State's other varsity teams participated in a special routine honoring the football team's motto, One Team. Then it was time for the Penn State alma mater, followed by "The Star-Spangled

A record crowd greets the Penn State football team in its traditional game-day arrival at Beaver Stadium before the first game of the 2012 season against Ohio University on September 1. Photo courtesy of John Beale

Banner." The band broke formation and formed two lines from the goal post to midfield for the players and coaches to run between. The other varsity student-athletes joined the lines carrying banners, and about 200 football lettermen got in the line too, along with the deans of the university's 11 colleges. "One Team."

The Jumbotrons showed the team leaving the locker room and walking into the tunnel toward the blue iron gate about 20 yards from the south goal posts. The screaming, yelling, and cheering got louder. When Bill O'Brien, followed by his players, ran through the band's two lines with the Lions mascot and cheerleaders leading the way, the crowd went wild, and the ensuing standing ovation lasted for minutes. The referee called the game captains to midfield for the kickoff as Penn State fans cheered "We Are…Penn State" several times. Ohio University won the coin toss and deferred. Penn State selected to defend the north goal, farthest away from the students.

ESPN cameras set the scene. And at 12:06 PM the 2012 season officially began. Linebacker Gerald Hodges took the ball at the goal line and got as far as the 12 before being tackled. Penn State fans had just seen the first surprise of the game. A linebacker is one of the kick returners.

That was Hodges' only kickoff return of the game, but he also returned two of the three Ohio punts. Tailback Bill Belton returned the other two Ohio kickoffs for 21 and 24 yards. After the game O'Brien said Hodges was one of "four or five guys" who ran back kicks in preseason practice.

By that time the fans had seen the names on the backs of the uniforms. My wife and I like them. We always sit high above the south end zone, almost directly behind the goalposts. I use binoculars, and like a thousand others inside the stadium, I listen to the Steve Jones–Jack Ham broadcast on the radio. Throughout the game I have always had to refer to player numbers in the game program. Except for some plays at the other end of the field, today I was able to read the names on their jerseys.

The opening six minutes were an indication of what followed in the next 54 minutes of today's game. Penn State drove 64 yards to Ohio's 24-yard line, but Belton fumbled on first down, and OU recovered.

Despite the fumble, this did not look like the offense loyal fans have been watching for the last few decades. It was wide-open, up-tempo, innovative, and bold. McGloin completed six of his first seven attempts to five different receivers, and with a fourth-and-1 at the

OU 48-yard line, O'Brien surprisingly went for it instead of punting, and McGloin completed an eight-yard pass to Kersey. Running always was the foundation of Paterno's conservative philosophy, and going for it on fourth down at midfield this early in the game, no matter if it was just inches, would have been blasphemous in the past. We soon found out that fourth down is now a crucial part of O'Brien's enterprising offense, just as he promised.

With three seconds left in the first quarter, Penn State took a 7–0 lead after an 80-yard drive. Just before halftime the Lions went ahead 14–3 after a punt blocked by freshman linebacker Nyeem Wartman at the OU 25-yard line set up a 14-yard touchdown pass from McGloin to redshirt junior tight end Matt Lehman.

But everything changed in the second half. Ohio took the kickoff and drove 82 yards to narrow the Lions' lead to 14–10, making what became the key play of the game. On a third-and-7 at the PSU 43-yard line, an ill-advised floater downfield by Ohio's quarterback was tipped into the receiver's hands after two Lions safeties collided, and he ran for the touchdown. Before the third quarter was over, Ohio had driven 70 yards on eight quick plays to take the lead, 17–14.

OU missed an opportunity to add to their lead when Matt Weller missed a 39-yard field goal early in the fourth quarter, then with 9:37 left in the game, Penn State had the visitors backed up to their own 7-yard line with a perfect opportunity to turn the game around. However, OU used up nearly seven minutes of the clock and methodically ground out 93 yards through the supposedly strong Lions defense for a touchdown that sealed the game.

Final score: 24–14. Statistics of the game: Ohio converted 13-of-21 third downs compared to Penn State's 8-of-16 and dominated time of possession 9:34 to 3:41 in the fourth quarter.

O'Brien quickly hustled to midfield for the customary handshake with the opposing coach and then ran toward the tunnel entrance with players ahead and behind him. He and the team never stopped at the student section to sing the alma mater.

Explaining this omission, Jordan Hill told reporters, "A lot of us, we forgot about it because it was something we've never done before. With everything else going on, it was something we overlooked by accident. It wasn't anything that, because we lost, we didn't want to do it."

O'Brien was wearing a Penn State ball cap for his first postgame news conference, marking the first time ever the head football coach has talked to reporters in the stadium media room with a hat on. Several in the media followed his lead and wore ball caps.

Was Joe Paterno turning over in his grave?

O'Brien was not in a good mood, and he cut off the questions after eight minutes. His answers were curt and defiant, sometimes one-word replies, and he was angry with himself as much as anyone. He said, "They beat us…. They were the better team…. We have to do better offensively, we have to get our defense off the field, and the defense has to make stops. We have to coach better, and it starts with me."

The players were upset with themselves, but they tried not to show their true emotions to the media.

"It was a bad performance by our unit as a whole, and you won't see that again," Hill told reporters. "We had a bad day today."

"We're going to put this behind us," said Mauti. "We're not going to let this carry over to next week or the week after that. It's a 12-game season."

"We couldn't make the plays when we needed to," said McGloin.

"A loss is a loss," said Stankiewitch, "but we have to stick together as a team, and that's what we are going to do. That's our focus for the season, and our focus for the next game."

This was supposed to be the game to get the beleaguered 2012 team off to a great start. Next Saturday's game at Virginia was expected to be the first tough one. Not only is the team now in a hole, but the fans feel they are there too. After all, they also have been disparaged by many in the media and by much of the public. Virginia now looks like a must-win.

There is also a question about fan support. The raucous crowd today was behind the team, but there were at least 10,000 or more empty seats. The announced crowd of 97,186 didn't account for all the no-shows. Even before the scandal, there had been much discontent over a new seat licensing policy implemented before the 2011 season that caused many season-ticket holders to either downsize their allotment of tickets or give them up altogether.

For the first time in years, there are thousands of season tickets still available. All the empty seats are not a good sign for the rest of the six home games. The NCAA sanctions are already costing the athletics department most of the money they once depended on to fund all the department's programs, projects, and staff. Fewer spectators is bad not only for Penn State but for the business community that relies on football Saturday weekends. "One Team" has meaning beyond the 2012 team.

Monday, September 3, 2012

Mauti and Zordich called a players-only meeting.

"We just felt like everybody needed to stay together and it was only one game on Saturday and we got 11 more to go," Mauti told Bob Flounders of the

(Harrisburg) Patriot-News. "We didn't want this to carry over into the week and affect our week of practice."

Tuesday, September 4, 2012

Everyone waited to see what O'Brien would say at his Tuesday press conference.

At his weekly news conference, O'Brien made no excuses for Saturday and reiterated that the team has to play better, convert more third-down plays, break up more passes, and complete more passes. "We did not make those plays, and Ohio did," he said, adding that he has to have a more balanced offense and better punting.

O'Brien noted that the injury to Belton's ankle in the Ohio game probably will mean Day, a former walk-on senior with limited playing time in 2001, will start at tailback at Virginia. O'Brien said he is preparing the team for the crowd noise because "it's a great home advantage for Virginia...a very, very difficult place to play." He warned that Virginia is a big, physical team with many veterans "that play extremely hard," with an offense "of motioning and shifting" that gives "a lot of different looks."

The most significant news in his news conference had nothing to do with either the Ohio or Virginia games. O'Brien revealed that Penn State will no longer refer to nonscholarship players as "walk-ons," the longtime standard college nomenclature. Henceforth, they will be known as "run-ons." "These guys don't walk, they run on the field, they sprint on the field, they bust their butt on the field," O'Brien explained. "[The run-on program is] something that we know is going to be important in the next few years.... Hopefully that resonates with kids in Pennsylvania especially."

O'Brien also disclosed he has given an official name to the scout team that prepares the rest of the team for game day. It will now be referred to as "the Dirty Show."

Wednesday, September 5, 2012

O'Brien brought an innovation to the Quarterback Club luncheon when he added video to his presentation before taking questions.

These were segments from the same video the team saw that week that broke down plays from the previous game as well as plays run by the next opponent. Working with a graduate assistant coach manning the video control board, O'Brien explained the plays, pointing out successful moves or mistakes by the offense, defense, and special teams.

The video was a big hit with the club members, most of whom had never seen this type of game-day video breakdown. These were not the usual game highlights that fans were accustomed to seeing, but more technical stuff familiar to players, coaches, and students of the game of football. As the weeks went by, just about all the attendees were into it, and O'Brien's video became almost as important to everyone as his answers to their questions.

Friday, September 7, 2012

A Penn State football team made its first road trip under a new head coach in 46 years, and two more rules from the Paterno era were changed. But O'Brien continued one longtime Paterno road-game custom when he socialized with reporters privately in the media hospitality room Friday evening. Most everything was off the record, and he told them of a major personnel move he had made for the next day's game. No one reported it until after the game.

Players no longer have to wear coats and ties for traveling. They are now wearing their travel warm-ups and tennis shoes. However, the coaches still have on coats and ties. Reporters at the hotel when the team buses arrived from the Charlottesville airport noticed some coaches' wives, including O'Brien's, in the group. Taking wives on these charter flights also was taboo in the past.

Saturday, September 8, 2012

Virginia, which beat Richmond, a Football Championship Subdivision team, 43–19 in its season opener, was a 10-point favorite in this ABC-televised game kicking off at noon. It was 83 degrees and cloudy as the kickoff neared, and temperatures were expected to rise, with severe thunderstorms possible before the end of the game.

Many of the Penn State fans in Charlottesville were concerned about a hostile crowd inside the stadium and in the tailgate lots, which for visitors are not close to the stadium. But the Virginia fans were friendly and gracious. There was a scattering of empty seats in the 61,000-seat stadium, and the official attendance later announced at 56,087 included an estimated 9,000 to 10,000 Penn State fans.

Virginia won the coin toss and deferred. Penn State's first possession was a coach's dream. The Lions went 75 yards in a near-perfect 17-play, six-and-a-half-minute drive that climaxed with an eight-yard touchdown pass from McGloin to redshirt freshman tight end Kyle Carter and an extra point by Ficken. It was a well-balanced attack with successful fourth-and-1 plays at the Penn State 45-yard line and Virginia's 45, with McGloin and Zordich each picking up the needed yardage.

O'Brien wisely punted on the Lions' next fourth-down opportunity late in the first quarter—a fourth-and-2 at their own 22-yard-line. However, on the Lions' first possession of the second quarter, with a fourth-and-4 at the Penn State 42-yard line, O'Brien called for a fake punt and a direct snap to the blocker, junior linebacker Glenn Carson, gained 19 yards. But the drive ended on another fourth-and-4 attempt five plays later when freshman backup quarterback Steven Bench, in the game because of an injury to McGloin, was sacked for a two-yard loss. But O'Brien backed up his promise to use the fourth down as just another opportunity to move the ball.

The defense's first opportunity appeared to be a coach's dream too. On the first play, at the Virginia 27-yard line after the kickoff, Mauti's hard tackle caused a fumble by the Virginia pass receiver that Obeng-Agyapong picked up and ran to the Virginia 17-yard line. The game clock showed 8:18 left in the first quarter, and from that point on, the game transformed from a coach's dream into a nightmare. On fourth down, Ficken trotted onto the field for a 40-yard field-goal attempt, and it was wide left. No one watching in the stadium or on television realized it, but they had not only seen the momentum of the game change for the next 51 minutes and 20 seconds, but also the player who would be blamed for it all by the fans.

Each team got 10 more possessions, and the last one for each determined the winner. Midway through the second quarter, Ficken missed a 38-yard field goal—wide right—after an interception by Jordan Hill, and Virginia followed with a 46-yard field goal before the first half ended. Virginia took the second-half kickoff and drove 77 yards to take the lead, 10–7. The Lions struck back with their own 72-yard drive, but Ficken's 20-yard field-goal attempt was wide right. Early in the fourth quarter, McGloin threw a 30-yard touchdown pass to Allen Robinson, but Ficken's extra-point attempt was blocked. Moments later, redshirt freshman defensive end Deion Barnes sacked the quarterback, forcing a fumble that Mauti recovered at the Virginia 17-yard line. Three plays later, Ficken trotted onto the field again as the Lions fans in the grandstands held their breath. His 32-yard field goal was good, and Penn State led 16–10 with 10:55 remaining in the game.

With 8:04 left Virginia got the ball on its own 14-yard line as a light rain began to fall, and in five plays had a third-and-16 on its own 22-yard line with five minutes remaining. The Lions defense forced Virginia's quarterback out of the pocket, but he passed toward a receiver drifting behind the Penn State secondary in three-deep coverage about 40 yards away. Obeng-Agyapong hit the receiver at almost the same time as the ball, but it was caught at the Penn State 34-yard line, and Obeng-Agyapong was flagged for interference. Virginia moved to the Penn State 7-yard line with 2:42 left as the stadium message board lit up with LIGHTNING IN THE AREA and many spectators headed for the exits. On third down Virginia scored a six-yard touchdown and the extra point that jumped Virginia into the lead, 17–16. The clock showed 1:28 remaining.

From the Penn State 27-yard line, McGloin confidently directed the Lions' two-minute offense in a steady rain, completing six-of-nine passes to four different receivers to reach the Virginia 22-yard line. The Lions lost three yards on a run and called timeout with one second remaining. On came Ficken for a 42-yard field-goal attempt. The field and the ball were wet, and the rain was heavier. Emery Etter's snap was a bit low, but holder Ryan Keiser grabbed the ball and set it down as Ficken's right leg moved forward. Wide left—far wide left.

Final score: 17–16. Statistics of the game: Penn State missed on four field-goal attempts and an extra point and did not score after three turnovers for minus-17 yards.

Coach O'Brien was disappointed but mellower than last week when he met with the media. Some highlights of that conference::

—"These kids left it all out there today, there's no question about that, and I really appreciate their effort…. We'll break through. We just have to do a better job in the red [zone] area offensively and stop people on third-and-long, and we have to keep fighting."

—"It's never always about the kicker; the kicker is always the one to get blamed, but it's the whole operation: the snap, the hold, the kick.... We need to see what things we can do to help Sam get better.... It's a team sport...I could have called better plays, we could have executed better."

— "I thought [the defense] played their tails off, and they did a lot of things really well. They got a bunch of turnovers, [gave up] a couple third-and-longs here and there, but they played very well.... We can't come away with no points with all those turnovers. That was a difference in the ballgame."

The team leaders agreed with their coach.

Mauti, who led the team in tackles again (with nine) and forced one fumble and recovered another said, "I was proud of our defense...it was a big improvement over last week."

"We told [Sam] to keep his head up," Stephon Morris said. "He didn't lose the game for us. It's not his fault."

"Sam did not lose this game whatsoever," said McGloin. "We missed other opportunities.... It kills you inside.... We're playing as hard as we can on the field, and it just kind of feels like something's stopping us.... We gotta fight through this. We've overcome so much in the past already, this is nothing compared to what we've been through."

The postgame news also revealed that Day, who started at tailback, is now out with an arm and elbow injury after being hit by a runner while standing on the sideline. That means there probably will be a third starting tailback against Navy. There almost was a new starting quarterback too. McGloin left the game late in the second quarter after twice banging his left elbow on a Virginia lineman's helmet. That led O'Brien to send in true freshman Steven Bench for the rest of the half, but after X-rays proved negative, McGloin was back for the second half with bandages wrapped around his sore elbow.

When Bench entered the game, the Penn State fans in the stands wondered why it wasn't Paul Jones, the designated backup, instead. O'Brien confidentially told the beat writers last night that he promoted Bench and moved Jones to the F-tight end position but that Jones will also continue to practice at quarterback too. Bench was on the field for 13 plays.

The last time Penn State started 0–2, in 2001, it finished 5–6. And it was Virginia defeating the Nittany Lions 20–14 in this same stadium, on a controversial 92-yard fumble return for a touchdown in the fourth quarter, that sealed the losing season on a 70-degree December 1 afternoon.

Two games in Scott Stadium in 12 years, and both have ended as frustrated defeats in games Penn State should have won. This is not a good omen for Bill O'Brien and his "One Team."

Charlie Mike! Charlie Mike!

Chapter 10

The Bleeding Stops

What happened next is indelibly seared into the hearts and minds of all Penn State football fans and made the 2012 football team honored forever as one of the greatest in school history.

When the players flew back after the exasperating loss to Virginia, their season could have gone either way. If they had finally given in to all the setbacks and obstacles that had already drained them emotionally, no one would have blamed them. After all, they were basically just older kids—some of them still teenagers, all of them straining to mature into full adulthood. In their young lives they already had encountered serious, stress-filled issues that tested their character. It would have been easy to back away. This was football, not life or death. Yet the words of a former Penn State player who faced death in combat were continuing to percolate in their hearts and minds. "Charlie Mike," Rick Slater, the Navy SEAL, had told them that evening in July—the day all those loyal fans came out at dawn to support them. "Charlie Mike"—Continue Mission. "Charlie Mike" was in their blood now, and "Charlie Mike" was the rallying cry. "Charlie Mike!" "One Team!"

The 2012 team had 10 games left after Virginia. Surprisingly, they were favored in all but two of them—Ohio State was a toss-up—and only lost one of them while beating the point spread in every game. They averaged 31.9 points per game in the final 10 games while giving up an average of 18.8 points.

The overpowering 38–14 victory at Iowa when Penn State was a three-point underdog was a shock, and the 35–7 victory at Illinois when the Lions were just a one-point favorite was not far behind. Only unbeaten Ohio State, who went on to finish No. 3 in the final Associated Press polls, outplayed Penn State, and the Lions held their own for the first 15 minutes, until Ohio State turned a 7–7 score after one quarter into a 35–23 victory. And at the end, the ultimate destiny of this "remarkable journey of the 2012 Nittany Lions" came down to a winning 37-yard field goal in overtime, on a cold and windy Thanksgiving Saturday weekend, kicked by the most maligned player of the first weeks of the season—19-year-old Sam Ficken.

Monday, September 10, 2012

The team resumed practice with greater determination and without any sense of panic. "We didn't have a come-to-Jesus meeting in that aspect among seniors or among players," tackle Mike Farrell told Scott Brown of the *Pittsburgh Tribune-Review* months later. "We just maintained the idea that we were just going to refuse to be denied."

Tuesday, September 11, 2012

Ficken's erratic kicking at Virginia was a prime subject at O'Brien's weekly news conference.

O'Brien was asked just one question about the team morale, and he answered, "I see the morale as really at a good level. The morale is really set by your seniors…. Football teaches you a lot about getting knocked down and being able to get back up and go back to work on a Monday after not being successful on a Saturday. These kids are tough kids. They've been through a lot, and they're really, really looking forward to practicing today and playing the game on Saturday.

"Sam's gotta do better in his technique, and he's really working on it. He must have kicked 300 kicks yesterday in practice…. You can see [on the video from the Virginia game] where the protection wasn't great, the snap wasn't always great, the hold wasn't always great, and so it's not always the kicker…. It's 10 guys doing a better job of protecting and Sam getting better at his overall technique."

O'Brien said Dukes will probably start at tailback on Saturday because of injuries to Belton and Day and said, "You'll see [redshirt sophomore Zach] Zwinak in there…you may even see [fullback] Michael Zordich do some things there."

O'Brien said the team has definitely improved from the first week, but they need to do better in the red zone, and he complimented McGloin for his progress as a leader: "He's gotten much better… in many ways he's grown up in the eight months since I've had him. He's done a really good job of huddle command and being encouraging to his teammates and playing tough, playing through some injuries." O'Brien emphasized the fourth down again, saying, "You can't just all of a sudden go for it…. [It has to be] a manageable fourth down…. You're also looking at the field position. So once we get really close to the 50, I'm pretty much not going to punt it."

Wednesday, September 12, 2012

Starting wide receiver Shawney left the team "for personal reasons" but remained enrolled in the university.

Thursday, September 13, 2012

Run-on redshirt freshman kicker/punter Matt Marcincin also quit the team "for personal reasons."

Friday, September 14, 2012

Penn State designated Saturday's game against Navy as Military Appreciation Day, and as part of the weekend activities, a memorial was dedicated today on Friday near Old Main in honor of Medal of Honor winner Lieutenant Michael P. Murphy and all veterans. Murphy was a 1998 Penn State graduate and Navy SEAL who was killed in the desolate mountains of Afghanistan in June 2005. Former SEAL team captain Ryan McCombrie, recently elected to the Penn State Board of Trustees, and ex-SEAL team commander Mark McGinnis, representing the Naval Academy, participated in the event and on Saturday would be honorary captains at the football game.

Saturday, September 15, 2012

Penn State football fans love days like this. The weather was perfect, with sunny skies and temperatures in the high 60s, and the tailgating started nine hours before the 3:40 PM kickoff. Navy had had two weeks to prepare for the game, after losing its season opener 50–10 in its traditional game against Notre Dame, played this year in a nontraditional location—Dublin, Ireland. Penn State had not played Navy since 1974, and the Lions were just a five-and-a-half-point favorite, partly because of the team's stumbling performance in its first two games and Navy's ball-control triple-option offense, which was unfamiliar to the Penn State defense.

When the Penn State team made its customary entrance running through the dual lines of the Blue Band, it was led by two players carrying the American flag: run-ons P.J. Byers and Brent Smith.

Gerald Hodges (No. 6) and Jordan Hill (No. 47) give Bill O'Brien a traditional Gatorade shower after the Nittany Lions defeated Navy 34–7, O'Brien's first win as head coach of the Penn State football team. Photo courtesy of Mark Selders, Penn State University Intercollegiate Athletic Archives

Byers, a senior fullback, is on active Naval duty. He is working on his degree and an officer commission through the ROTC after spending three years to become a navy diver specializing in underwater submarine repair and demolitions. Smith is a 26-year-old freshman who had two tours of duty in Iraq before trying out for the team at defensive end.

As the kickoff approached, two navy F/A-28 Super Hornet jets flew over the stadium to the cheers of the crowd, which included a small corps of Naval Academy Midshipmen and members of Penn State's three ROTC units—the most such components for any nonmilitary school in the nation.

Penn State won the toss and, surprisingly, elected to receive, but the reason was to keep Navy's possession offense off the field. Adrian Amos ran the kickoff back to the 28-yard line, and as the ESPN2/ABC TV audience watched, a 45-yard pass to Allen Robinson set up a two-yard touchdown reception by true freshman tight end Jesse James. Ficken's PAT makes it 7–0. With 6:40 left in the quarter, Robinson scored a touchdown on a 45-yard pass reception, and Ficken's kick pushed the lead to 14–0.

Although nobody knew it, the game was basically over at this juncture. Penn State possessed the ball just six more times but scored three more touchdowns on two touchdown passes of two and 25 yards from McGloin to Robinson and a 75-yard return of a fumble by redshirt sophomore linebacker Mike Hull. The Lions were ahead 34–0 before Navy finally scored early in the fourth quarter.

Final score: 34–7. Statistics of the game: Statistics are deceiving, as Navy dominated the major statistics except for passing yardage, including time of possession (36:23 to 23:37) and number of plays (83 to 49).

McGloin finished the game with 13-of-21 completions for 231 yards and four touchdowns, while Zordich, who was the starting running back, had the best day of his career so far as the Lions' leading rusher with 50 yards on 11 carries. With Mauti once again leading the way with 12 tackles, Penn State recorded four turnovers on three fumbles and an interception and made four sacks, including Mauti's first of the season. But Ficken still had a problem, missing an extra point, which might have been the reason O'Brien later bypassed a 25-yard field goal at the Navy 8-yard line for a pass that was incomplete.

Before the game ended, O'Brien was given a Gatorade drenching by his players. After the customary handshake at midfield, O'Brien and the players joined the Navy team, and they walked together to the northeast corner of the stadium, where Navy sang its familiar alma mater with its fans. Then both teams strolled to the southeast corner of the end zone where, arm-in-arm, the Lions players and O'Brien sang the Penn State alma mater with the students and Blue Band before they headed toward the tunnel and individually rang the traditional victory bell—the first for O'Brien.

What the fans didn't see was the locker-room scene that the athletics department's video specialist, Tony Mancuso, shot after today's game [see appendix]. As the players filed into the locker room, O'Brien greeted each with a handshake, pat, or hug. Then he called them all together and told them, "Great job, but that's just one. Only one," as he pointed his finger into the air several times. He said, "We gotta get ready for Temple. That's just one. What I told you last night is this can start a roll, if we keep staying together and practice together the way we've been practicing. Let's get this thing going the right way and keep it going." Then Zordich presented O'Brien with the game ball, and everyone cheered.

O'Brien was smiling when he met with the media. "The one thing that winning does is it cures a lot of things," he said. "Winning also breeds confidence…all of the hard work [the players] put in this week and past weeks paid off…. Like I've said from day one, there's nothing that any of us can do about the NCAA. All we can do is play under the rules…that's what we're doing, and these kids have really stuck together."

O'Brien complimented his offense and defense and, when questioned, had nice things to say about several players, including

McGloin, Zordich, Robinson, redshirt freshman defensive end Deion Barnes, and Paul Jones, who made a seven-yard catch on the drive for the third touchdown. The coach told reporters he hasn't lost confidence in Ficken, saying the pass play instead of the field goal was a good call, but "we blew the protection."

The players are relieved to have their first victory, and they said after the game that they especially wanted to win for their coach. "It felt good to just get a win for him," Hill told reporters. "And for us too. For all the hard work that we've put in and everything we've been through."

Zordich said, "We needed a win to get rolling."

Stankiewitch said, "[It's] a lot of weight off our shoulders," and Mauti echoed that, adding, "To get that first win kind of gets the monkey off our back a little bit."

The announced crowd was 98,792. The Penn State fans among them couldn't have been happier, unless they had seen Ficken kick a couple of field goals and not miss another extra point. But as they left the stadium and tailgated into the darkness, many wondered why O'Brien had not inserted his freshman quarterback into the game in the fourth quarter when there was no chance of a Navy comeback.

Tuesday, September 18, 2012

Another of the weekly press conferences with O'Brien. Only this one under much happier circumstances: the first win of the 2012 season! But thoughts had already turned to the Temple game, which was only four days away.

O'Brien told reporters he did not play Bench against Navy because "I felt like it was still a ballgame there. I know what the scoreboard said, but I just felt like it was still Matt's game, and I stuck with Matt there." He also said he should have used Paul Jones at tight end more, adding, "He's a team player, [and] he loves Penn State."

O'Brien said he's not overly concerned with the tailback position, despite injuries to his first two starting tailbacks: "It's a very, very physical position…. We're fortunate here at Penn State because we have a decent amount of guys there. They all do something a little bit different [and] can really play. It's more like we said from day one, it's the next man up."

Since the team has yet to score a rushing touchdown, he said, "We're definitely looking for improvement in the running game…. The offensive line has done a really good job of run blocking for the most part. It's probably more me having to call more runs."

The coach continues to have faith in Ficken but said all the kicking, including punting, needs to be more consistent: "Overall, special teams has [sic] been pretty good. Sam just needs to continue to get better at his technique." He also complimented the defense and said the coaches will continue to emphasize turnover ratio, saying, "If you don't turn the ball over and the other team turns the ball over, you have a better chance to win."

At least one or more questions about Mauti is now part of each of these weekly news conferences. Today O'Brien said, "I just can't say enough about Mike Mauti. He's just a fantastic guy…[and] has meant a lot to this football program, to this team, to his teammates. He's great in the locker room…. He just plays every play like it's his last play…. He's a guy that means a lot to me and means a lot to our football program."

Although Temple has lost 29 straight to Penn State since 1941, the last two games were close, and O'Brien said he expects a tough game: "They play at a very fast tempo; they take advantage of their players' skill sets. It's going to be a real big challenge for our defense on Saturday." O'Brien would not say much about Temple players calling this game their Super Bowl, only, "I'm glad it's their Super Bowl, but this is a big game for us, like every single game this year."

Friday, September 21 and Saturday, September 22
Penn State's 1982 team that won the school's first national championship was being honored this weekend, highlighted by the introduction of each returning player during halftime ceremonies of the Temple game.

The center of the team, Mark Battaglia, invited my wife and me to the team's private pregame tailgate in a large tent near the stadium. The place was filled with players and their families, and also included football lettermen from other years, including Steve Smear, cocaptain of the great undefeated back-to-back teams in 1968–69, and Rich Mauti, Michael's father. I had a special conversation about Ficken with Massimo Manca, the freshman place-kicker on the '82 team who also kicked for the second national championship team in 1986. "All kickers have bad periods," Manca told me. "No matter how much you practice or what you do, you can't seem to snap out of it. Then it just happens. Like that. And you wonder what finally did it. That will happen to the kid. It's just a matter of time."

Saturday, September 22, 2012
A "Blue Out" was declared, partially to recognize the seriousness of child-abuse problems, and most of the announced crowd of 93,680 showed up wearing blue T-shirts and sweatshirts for the 3:30 game televised by ABC and ESPN2.

It was a cloudy day with temperatures in the low 70s and rain expected. Penn State was a nine-point favorite. Some beat reporters warned this could be a "trap game," with the players having a letdown between their emotional victory against Navy and the Big Ten opener at Illinois, a foe they despised because of the egregiously unethical recruiting behavior by the Illini coaching staff in July.

Penn State lost the coin toss, and the game did not start well as Penn State's offense sputtered in its first two possessions. But with about 12 seconds left in the first quarter, Penn State was at the Temple 41-yard line with a fourth-and-5, and McGloin shocked Temple with a 41-yard touchdown pass to Robinson. Ficken's PAT made it 7–0, and Temple never caught up.

Early in the second quarter, Temple kicked a 33-yard field goal as a light rain began. Then, with time running out in the half, Butterworth's punt to the Temple 7-yard line and a forced punt by the defense set up a quick Penn State drive from the Owls 35-yard line. Two passes to Carter and a personal foul put the ball at the 1-yard line. From the shotgun formation, McGloin scored on a broken play with 0:22 remaining when Zordich went the wrong direction and McGloin dashed to his right and carried the defensive left end over the goal line with him from three yards out. Ficken kicked the extra point, and Temple never got closer.

The rain let up in the second half, and the sun came out again, in time to shine on the Nittany Lions. Penn State added to its lead with an 80-yard drive climaxed by another touchdown for McGloin and Ficken's PAT with 4:57 left in the third quarter. The teams traded field goals before Temple scored against Penn State's reserves in the last two minutes of the game.

Final score: 24–13. Statistics of the game: Penn State's defense held Temple to just 3-of-12 third-down conversions and dominated possession 36:52 to 23:08.

McGloin had a career day in passing yardage with 318 yards on 24-of-36 passes (to nine different receivers), while Zordich, starting at fullback again, had his own career day with 75 yards rushing on 15 carries, his longest run ever at Penn State, for 16 yards and four pass receptions for 39 yards. However, O'Brien may have found his new starting tailback as Zwinak came off the bench with Dukes nursing an injury and rushed for 94 yards on 18 carries. Robinson's five receptions for 82 yards will make him the leading receiver in the Big Ten just as the Lions get set to open their Big Ten schedule. With nine more tackles that led the team, Mauti will be second in Big Ten tackles with 41. The defense played its best game of the season by limiting Temple to 237 net yards with three sacks, one by Mauti. But penalties—nine for 100 yards, including a couple of offensive penalties for holding and illegal procedure—cost the Lions potential points, and that sort of play could be devastating in the Big Ten.

In the media room, O'Brien complained about the penalties and failures to score inside the 10-yard line: "I was disappointed in [the number of penalties]. We have to do a better job on that. We had lineman penalties, holding calls, and offensive pass interference…. After the first three games [we were proud of] doing a good job of not being penalized. Today, I felt like we took a step back on that… we had a productive day but we left a lot of points off the board…. When we have a chance to score inside the 10-yard line, we've got to do a better job…. It starts with coaching…. But I thought overall that the effort was good."

O'Brien was asked about McGloin and Zordich and said, "Matt is a very much improved quarterback. He's making good decisions with the ball. He's a fun guy to coach because he's a smart guy. He gets it after you tell him once. He's competitive, and he can keep his poise, sometimes better than I can…. Mike is a football player…. When he was learning the fullback position, he was trying to learn the whole package. That's what we tell our guys at every position. You cannot just know your own position. He has been a guy who has really worked at it."

O'Brien went on to credit the senior class, again, for the continued improvement in the team and for a strong winning attitude: "These guys know that they only have eight games left. They practice hard, they work hard, and they really care about each other…. [They're] a bunch of really resilient, tough kids that love to play football and love to go to school at Penn State…. They get along, there's good camaraderie."

When it was their turn, some of the leaders said Temple got them hyped up by referring to the game as their Super Bowl, but they talked more about how anxious they are to start their Big Ten schedule. "Getting two wins and being on a winning streak going into Big Ten is big," said Hill, "because [we] know the Big Ten is up for grabs and we can still win the Leaders Division."

Stankiewitch said winning two straight has given the team confidence: "We did not want to go into our Big Ten opener with a loss, but we needed this win and are very determined and focused on Illinois."

Media coverage of the game hardly mentioned Illinois, although some stories included a quote or two from a player. Even the postgame tailgaters didn't talk much about Illinois, perhaps because the game is away and few of these tailgaters will be making the trip. Another reason could be that most fans don't realize the intensity of the players' dislike for the Illinois coaching staff.

There was one downside for today's game. The announced attendance of 93,680 was the smallest official Beaver Stadium crowd since November 18, 1995. That's when an estimated 80,000 fans were there to see Penn State beat Michigan 27–17, despite snow piled under the seats, along the sidelines, and in many parking lots following a surprise 17½-inch snowfall four days earlier. With so many empty seats visible today and no disclosure of the number of no-shows, the number of actual spectators in the stadium was definitely much lower.

This also was the first game in which O'Brien made only one use of a fourth-down play to gain yardage, and that gave Penn State its first touchdown. In four games, the Lions have made 7-of-10 such fourth-down attempts and are now third in the nation behind Oregon and Louisiana-Monroe.

And Massimo Manca was almost right about Ficken. Ficken was perfect on his three extra-point attempts and his only field-goal try today, but he still needs to improve his kickoffs. A perfect kickoff is into the end zone for a touchback with no chance of a return. Ficken had one touchback, while the others were taken by Temple between the 3- and 10-yard lines. At least he stopped the bleeding too, just like the rest of his teammates.

Chapter 11

Revenge Is Sweet

Tuesday, September 25, 2012

The game against Illinois on September 29 had become a very hot-button topic, given U of I's legal but unprofessional behavior in trying to poach players from Penn State's roster.

Not only did O'Brien shy away from mentioning a special incentive to beat Illinois, but the players made available for interviews during the week tried to soft-pedal any revenge factor too. "As a football player, you use any type of motivation to get you going," said Hill.

Of interest, Mauti, the most vocal player who always speaks his mind, was off-limits to the media.

At his weekly news conference today, Bill O'Brien downplayed three questions—including the first one, from senior beat reporter Rich Scarcella, about being extremely motivated for the Illinois game because of the summer recruiting mischief by its coaching staff. "It takes a lot to bother me," he said. "The motivation is, it's our first Big Ten game on the road…. Our players are very focused on the Big Ten schedule…[and] on building on what they did well in the Temple game and improving in areas where we really need to improve. They're not concerned with anything other than playing a tough road game in Champaign against a good Illinois team."

The rest of the questions covered the usual gamut of subjects, such as appraisal of individual players, evaluation of Penn State's strengths and needs, a short analysis of the opponent and, as always, at least one inquiry about his relationship with players. The highlights:

—After utilizing the no-huddle offense a little bit in the first four games, O'Brien said, "We'll have a no-huddle game plan going into every game, and the flow of the game basically determines how much you're going to use no-huddle." He said McGloin is the key to making it work: "One of the things in playing quarterback in a system like ours is we put a lot on your plate…and you have to have a good deal of brainpower and you have to be able to understand what you're watching on film and be able to take that to the practice field and then take it to the game field. Every week he's improved on what he sees and getting us into the right play and using little tricks of the trade to help himself to get us into the right play."

—O'Brien said he can now depend on five players to run the ball but admitted it is too tough to use everyone in a game: "I definitely see us using two or three. Depends how they practice during the week…. Some guys are first- and second-down guys; some are three-down guys; some are a little bit quicker; some guys are bigger; some guys are faster; some guys catch the ball better."

—He said the defense has to prepare for two Illinois quarterbacks with different styles and added, "The Illinois defensive line is a big strength for their football team."

Wednesday, September 26, 2012

With rumors swirling all day, O'Brien confirmed after practice that Paul Jones had left the team. Jones used Twitter to say, "thank you to everyone that has reached out to me offering their support. I really appreciate it. My dream is playing quarterback. And I'm going to chase it."

Jones' departure moved rarely used senior Shane McGregor up to No. 3 quarterback, and O'Brien later had Belton, who played quarterback in high school, spend some practice time at the position.

Friday, September 28, 2012

On the eve of the game at Champaign, Penn State's beat reporters began posting predictions on their various websites.

Despite what O'Brien and the players have said publicly about any extra motivation, many reporters aren't quite buying it. In an online chat with his readers, Joe Julian of the *Philadelphia Inquirer* wrote, "The Nittany Lions open their Big Ten schedule on Saturday at Illinois. Of course, the subplot is the fact that coaches from the Fighting Illini staff came to State College in July shortly after the NCAA handed out its harsh sanctions to recruit Penn State players. If coaches and players are still angry about this, then they're doing a good job of hiding it."

At the beginning of the week, Penn State was a two-and-a-half-point favorite, but the public was still wary of what the sanction-depleted Lions could do against their more formidable Big Ten competition. By today, Illinois was a one-point favorite, despite being blown out in two of its four games, 45–14 at Arizona State and 52–24 last week at home against Louisiana Tech. Few in the media—even their own beat reporters—think Illinois will win, and Penn State's reporters are nearly unanimous in picking PSU, although their victory margins vary widely from one to 21 points, with a consensus somewhere in the middle. A sampling:

Mark Brennan, FightOnState.com: "I think the Lions will be playing with a little extra motivation against Illinois, at least as long as the classless Tim Beckman can hang on to the job." Score prediction: 27–13.

Bob Flounders, *(Harrisburg) Patriot-News*: "This one is personal for Penn State's football program." Score prediction: 20–17.

Nate Bauer, *Blue White Illustrated*: "There is an undeniable extra motivation for this game, both from the players and the Penn State coaching staff, regardless of whatever they're saying publicly about not holding a grudge and having more important things to worry about." Score prediction: 24–13

Colleen Kane, *Chicago Tribune*: "Both coaches downplayed this week Illinois' recruitment of Penn State players over the summer, but fans still will be watching for signs of hostility between the programs. Penn State is on the upswing after two straight victories, and the rise looks like it will continue in Champaign." Score prediction: 21–17

Saturday, September 29, 2012

There was plenty of room for parking in the public tailgating lots near Memorial Stadium and lot of empty seats inside as the 11:00 AM kickoff approached for the nationally televised ESPN game in the 70,904-seat stadium.

The fans who showed up saw one of the great plays in Penn State football history, for which Mauti two days later would be selected the Walter Camp Football Foundation's National Defensive Player of the Week.

The announced attendance of 46,734 included what would turn out to be the smallest contingent of Penn State fans for any of the five away games. Just 725 tickets were sold by the Penn State athletics department, but those ticket holders did get to see the Penn State Blue Band. The band is allowed to travel to only one away game during the regular season, and this year the Illinois game was it. So in reality, this was also the band's bowl game. I'm not sure they picked the right game, but for my wife and me and the other 723 fans that were there, revenge was sweet.

Even with a new coach, Illinois fans have soured on their team in the last two years, and when today's game was over, the reason was obvious. About the only thing the home team won was the opening coin toss.

In the last four Lions games, they scored twice on their first possession and reached the opponent's 24-yard and 45-yard lines in the other games. This time, however, it was three-and-out and a 47-yard punt from their own 31-yard line. Just as the punt returner was about to catch the ball, he saw Mauti roaring toward him, lost his concentration, and dropped the ball a second before Mauti smashed into him. Penn State's new long-snapper, run-on senior Mitch Furman, who played last week for the first time in his five years on the team, recovered at the Illini 26-yard line. On fourth-and-3 at the Illini 7-yard line, Ficken's field-goal attempt went awry, but Illinois was penalized for roughing the kicker. Two plays later Zwinak bashed over left tackle for the touchdown and Ficken's PAT. A few minutes later McGloin scored on a one-yard quarterback sneak after a 60-yard drive. With six and a half minutes to go in the first quarter, Penn State led 14–0.

But the offense sputtered and both teams missed field goals—Ficken's was wide left from 47 yards—before the Lions went 72 yards for a touchdown on a 21-yard pass reception by tight end Matt Lehman with 3:11 left in the half. Ficken's PAT stretched the lead to 21–0, but the play of the game was still about three minutes away.

Illinois drove 74 yards to the Penn State 4-yard line with 19 seconds remaining before the half. What happened next will be remembered as one of the greatest plays in Penn State football history. An Illini receiver appeared to be open over the middle, just across the goal line, but Mauti snatched the ball out of the air and ran down the sideline, past the Illinois bench. Just as he neared the goal line, he was tackled from behind and ruled down at the 1-yard line. The play was reviewed in the press box and confirmed. With one second left, Ficken tried an 18-yard field goal, but it was blocked. As the teams headed through the same tunnel to their dressing rooms, there was a little pushing and shoving.

Early in the third quarter, a tricky 22-yard halfback option pass gave Illinois a touchdown, but with 3:15 left in the third quarter, McGloin scored from the 2-yard line on a quarterback sneak, and with Ficken's kick it became a 21-point margin again. Penn State scored once more near the start of the fourth quarter, and on the last play of the game, the defense put an exclamation point on their vengeful victory as the Lions reserves stopped Illinois on a first-and-goal at the 1-yard line to end an 87-yard drive and a depressing day for Illini coach Tim Beckman.

Final score: 35–7. Statistics of the game: Total domination by the Nittany Lions as they won just about every category, and for the first time all year, Penn State called far more running plays than passes (52 to 30) with both Zwinak (19 carries for 100 yards) and Belton (16 carries for 65 yards) having the best days of their careers.

As the opposing head coaches ran toward the middle of the field for the traditional handshake, O'Brien brushed by Beckman, hardly touching his hand and without looking at him.

Many of the postgame comments from the players and some from O'Brien were about Mauti. Several players told Donnie Collins of the *Scranton Tribune* and others that before the game Mauti "stalked the locker room like a man possessed, screaming—sometimes to himself—and gazing toward the door, as if he couldn't wait for the moment it would open so he could be unleashed on the Illini."

"That was the craziest I've ever seen him," said Stephon Morris. "He was amped. I don't know what he was on, but he was banging his head against the locker and all this other stuff…. He had the defense going before the game, the whole game on the sideline, after the game. He was on."

Mauti admitted he was pumped beforehand and ecstatic in the locker room: "Playing against these guys was sweet. That's really what it was. We never forgot about what happened back in the summer, and to be honest with you, we had that in the back of our minds. That kept us going, and like I said, it was sweet."

O'Brien said Mauti isn't shy about what he says. "Any time you have things to say, it's very important to go out there and back it up," O'Brien told reporters. "That's what life is all about, really. He's a guy that doesn't have a lot of problems backing things up."

However, Mauti wasn't completely pleased. "Ninety-nine yards without a touchdown, yeah, that one's going to hurt," he said. "That one is going to haunt my dreams, especially when we didn't get any points out of it." (Mauti's run broke the school record for the longest interception return, previously established by linebacker Wayne Berfield against Boston University in 1958—a game that I covered for the *Daily Collegian*.)

O'Brien took the blame for not calling a running or pass play to get the points because he misjudged the yard line. He said, "We have to execute better on the field goal, but on the 1-yard line, we've got to be able to punch it in there."

The coach didn't want to talk about his so-called postgame handshake. "It's a Big Ten win," he said. "It's a really big win for us to get off on the right foot in the Big Ten. These games are not easy. This conference is tough, so any time you can get off on the right foot that's a big deal. Overall, it was a good team effort...[but] we left a lot of points off the board. We're gonna have to play a lot better [in the conference games]."

O'Brien also came up with a new name for what everyone else called the no-huddle offense. He referred to it as "our NASCAR package."

Zordich didn't play today because of a leg injury he suffered in the second half of the Temple game. Luckily, he wasn't missed.

Tuesday, October 2, 2012

It was obvious from this day's press conference that Bill O'Brien was not getting over confident after the team's convincing victory over Illinois but was deeply entrenched in plotting for the following week's game against Northwestern.

O'Brien's weekly news conference had a different tone today, and the coach seemed more relaxed. A couple of reporters asked for evaluations of backup players, and there were several questions concerning secondary issues. The only question about the Illinois victory was about the blocked field goal at the end of Mauti's late-first-half 99-yard interception return. "We had a tackle-over situation where, when we were kicking inside the 10-yard line, we put our tackle over [to the long side] because of the angle of the kick when it's on a hash [mark]," O'Brien replied. "[Illinois] blocked it from the long side. That didn't make me very happy."

O'Brien explained how his running back situation has changed with five backs—Belton, Zwinak, Zordich, Duke, and Day: "We have got some good guys back there, and it's really competitive in practice.... Nobody is going to carry it 30 times for us. It's more about that 10 to 15 carry range, probably, right now. Things change as the season goes on."

Northwestern, unbeaten in five games, is going to be a challenge, O'Brien said, and especially because of its rotating quarterbacks—one of whom often stays in the game as a wide receiver. He said the Lions have to practice for different formations and plays, depending on who's quarterbacking: "You have to communicate very well...[and] make sure you're lined up at the snap of the ball, because they are going to play very, very fast, and they are going to try to run 90 to 100 plays in the game.... Northwestern is the best team that we have faced."

Thursday, October 4, 2012

Bill O'Brien made his first appearance at Nittanyville and brought pizzas for the dozens of campers. Among the group of senior players who joined him were Mauti, Zordich, McGloin, Stankiewitch, and Farrell. "Be in there at noon ready to go, standing up, be loud, especially when Northwestern is on offense," O'Brien exhorted the students. "That will really disrupt what they do on offense. Be really loud throughout the whole game.... The student section means a ton to our players."

Saturday, October 6, 2012

This was the traditional Homecoming game to honor returning alumni, and the earliest in the calendar year since 2003, when the Lions lost 30–23 to Wisconsin.

For today's game, the students scheduled a "White Out," a once-or-twice-a-year special game day tradition that has become popular with the Penn State fans, who wear white clothing that ostensibly makes them cheer louder than usual. White Outs are not officially sanctioned by Penn State, which for legal reasons has to call its occasional dress-in-white games "White Houses." Although a White Out and a White House are virtually identical, the term "White Out" was copyrighted by the NHL Phoenix Coyotes when the franchise was known as the Winnipeg Jets in 1987. However, it's okay for students to schedule a White Out, because it's not officially endorsed by the university. Seems silly to me, but that's the legal interpretation.

Northwestern came in ranked No. 22 in the USA Today/ESPN Top 25 and No. 24 in the AP Top 25, and along with AP No. 12 Ohio State, was one of only two unbeaten teams in the Big Ten. Northwestern also had an extra incentive. They were striving for the team's first 6–0 start since 1962. Today was expected to be a high-scoring but close game. But when they kicked off before the ESPN cameras shortly after noon, as the sun finally broke through what had been a dreary, cool, and wet morning, Penn State was a three-point favorite. And unlike last Saturday at Illinois, this game always has a friendlier atmosphere because of the respect the schools, players, coaches, and alumni usually have for each other.

Penn State won the coin toss and chose to receive. The style of this game was completely different from Penn State's first five. After the kickoff, the teams traded short punts before Ficken kicked a 21-yard field goal following a short 33-yard drive. The Lions made it 10–0 six minutes into the second quarter on another short drive of 40 yards, primarily on the running of Zwinak, who got the touchdown on a one-yard run. Penn State seemed to be in control, but midway through the second quarter a fumbled punt at the Lions 17-yard line led to a Northwestern touchdown. Then with 2:20 left in the half, Northwestern quickly went 66 yards on eight passing plays and a questionable third-down interference penalty on Morris to take a 14–10 lead as the half ended.

For the first time this season, the Lions were behind at the intermission, and the crowd watching Homecoming's traditional halftime ceremonies featuring the Blue Band and the Alumni Blue Band was nervous. Penn State took the lead again early in the third quarter on an 80-yard drive, but Northwestern retaliated immediately with its own 71-yard march to take it back. That led to the play that could have spoiled the season for the 2012 team. Northwestern forced a punt and returned it 75 yards for a touchdown with 50 seconds left in the third quarter, the first punt return for a TD Penn State had given up since the 2006 Orange Bowl.

On the sideline the coaches and players were once again encouraging each other to get back on the field. As Paterno used to tell these and all his players, you really don't know how good your team is until they are behind in the fourth quarter and in trouble. These were now O'Brien's players, but they were originally molded under Paterno's perceptive philosophy, and this was just one more hitch in the unprecedented and challenging season. Northwestern never had a chance.

In the fourth quarter, Penn State drove 82, 85, and 28 yards for touchdowns while stopping the Wildcats twice on three-and-outs. The Lions capped the 39–28 victory when Hodges forced a fumble at the Northwestern 41 with 0:44 left in the game.

Final score: 39–28. Statistics of the game: Penn State dominated the statistics, including time of possession (39:17 to 20:43), plays (99 to 61), net yardage (443 to 247), first downs (30 to 14), third-down conversions (10-of-22 vs. 4-of-13), and fourth-down conversions (5-of-6 vs. 0-of-1).

After the friendly handshakes at midfield by O'Brien and his players, the team headed straight to the student section to sing the alma mater, and then O'Brien ran along the wall of the student section high-fiving students as the players walked toward the tunnel and took their turns ringing the victory bell.

"You can't say enough about these kids," O'Brien said in the media room when asked about the fourth-quarter comeback. "I did sense [them being down] a little for a few seconds there after the punt return…. We tried to get our players going…. We had another quarter to play, and we felt we could move the ball…. These guys are playing hard and it's really fun to see the smiles on their faces."

O'Brien said his NASCAR offense has been "effective pretty much all year," and he credits McGloin: "Up-tempo is good, our players seem to enjoy it…they look forward to the up-tempo game plan every week. Matt does a nice job of handling the plays there: the tempo, the situations, knowing the down and distance."

Neither O'Brien nor Northwestern Coach Pat Fitzgerald would talk about an argument they had when O'Brien went on the field to chastise the officials after the controversial interference call on Morris that led to Northwestern's late-second-quarter go-ahead touchdown. But some players did. "Everyone is our rivals," Morris said coyly. "We really have no friends in this conference. The whole Big Ten [Network] crew had us losing this game. We just want to prove [ourselves] to the world each and every week." Zordich said, "We might not be able to play for a bowl game or a national championship, but we're still hungry and still have a lot to prove."

So, the visiting alumni who can only attend one home game a year celebrated in the parking lots with their peers and other fans among the season-ticket holders. But neither Homecoming nor the exciting product on the field are the attraction they once were. The announced attendance was 95,769, but ESPN showed many empty seats. It's too bad, because this has become a special team, and they are making Penn State alumni everywhere proud.

Sunday, October 7 to Saturday, October 13, 2012

Penn State's football team had its Big Ten bye week. There were lighter practices the first three days to refresh the players and give more time for injuries to heal before they turned their attention another rival that had become Penn State's prime nemesis in the past 12 years—Iowa.

Monday, October 8, 2012

Michael Mauti was not included in the list of 25 quarterfinalists for the Lombardi Award, given to the college football outstanding linebacker or lineman. Not only were Penn State beat reporters surprised but so were some members of the national media, wondering if Mauti was being penalized because of the Sandusky scandal.

A couple other tidbits on this day:

Penn State led the country in fourth-down attempts and successful conversions with 13-for-20.

McGloin was No. 1 in the Big Ten in passing yardage per game (249.8) and completions (136) and was tied for the lead with 12 touchdown passes, with just two interceptions. He had had four straight 200-yard passing games and five for the season.

Tuesday, October 9, 2012

Saturday's convincing win over Northwestern impressed the national media, and Bill O'Brien was beginning to get touted as a serious possibility for Coach of the Year.

Dennis Dodd of CBSSports.com tweeted today, "Going to go ahead and say it since PSU is off next week. Halfway through the season, Bill O'Brien. Coach. Of. The. Year."

There was no weekly news conference at the stadium today, but in his shorter session with reporters as part of the Big Ten's weekly coaches' teleconference, O'Brien said the Coach of the Year talk is the "farthest thing from my mind. We're 4–2 and we have murderers' row coming up here, starting with Iowa. There's a lot of great coaches in this country. I've only coached six games my whole career."

O'Brien said last week that he liked "the fact that the bye week comes in the middle of the season," and today he told reporters, "We're going to really spend a lot of time on special teams…areas of special teams have struggled, but really it's the specialists that have struggled. The kickers, punters, and snapper…. I think our specialists need to play better, but overall our kids on special teams have done good things."

Penn State's beat reporters agree with O'Brien about the last six games. "The Lions are about to take on the meat of their Big Ten schedule," wrote Bob Flounders of the *(Harrisburg) Patriot-News*. "At Iowa. Then home against No. 8 Ohio State. Followed by consecutive road games against Purdue and Nebraska. And the two home games against Indiana and Wisconsin. Certainly a challenging stretch… [but] given PSU's improvement in the last month, I'm certain that the Lions' final six opponents are more than a little nervous about facing the Lions' team that has won four straight. Because this is a different team than the one that started the season 0–2."

Monday, October 14, 2012

Midway through the college football season, six Penn State players continued to be on the "watch list" for major awards at their position, including Mauti for the Butkus and Bednarik linebacker trophies. The others were seniors Jordan Hill: Outland (offensive and defensive linemen) and Lombardi; Hodges: Butkus, Bednarik, Lombardi, and Nagurski (defensive player); Stankiewitch: Rimington (center); sophomore Allen Robinson: Biletnikoff (wide receiver); and redshirt freshman Kyle Carter: Mackey (tight end).

Tuesday, October 15, 2012

This Tuesday saw a return to O'Brien's weekly news conferences. The media wanted to hear about the team's bye-week activities and their strategy for their meeting with Iowa in four days.

At today's press conference, O'Brien was asked about the player awards and admitted he doesn't know much about them. But he said, "I don't think any of these guys here really care about individual awards. These are a bunch of competitive guys that love being a part of a team. They're team players…they would tell you we just want to win because that's what they're all about."

In response to another question about a possible stigma attached to Penn State, O'Brien replied, "I would certainly hope not. This is a special place with a bunch of tough, hard-nosed kids that go to class and do things the right way and play as hard a football as they can play.... We have got a very, very tough schedule coming up, and I'm proud of these players, and I just think that they should be given that chance to be recognized just like every other player."

Questions about Iowa monopolized the news conference, and O'Brien said: "[Iowa's] an excellent...football team that plays a physical brand of football...that's very, very well coached. They know what they want to do. They do it well.... They're a smart team. They don't make a lot of mistakes, if any.... Iowa has the momentum because they had a fantastic win [last Saturday] over a very tough Michigan State team in double overtime.... [Kinnick Stadium is] a very difficult place to play, as are most of the places in the Big Ten. It's going to be an electric atmosphere. Crowd noise is definitely going to be a factor.... I think it's two very, very evenly matched teams that are going to really fight it out physically to see who can win the game."

O'Brien also talked about how he and Iowa's head coach, Kirk Ferentz—the longest-tenured head coach in the Big Ten, with 14 years—and his son Brian, an assistant, are all part of the Bill Belichick coaching tree. He said, "I'm close with Brian.... I obviously have a lot of respect for his dad and what he's done at the University of Iowa."

Someone asked about a comment Stephon Morris made Monday night via a tweet—"we hate them, they hate us"—that already was creating some controversy in Iowa. O'Brien replied: "Do you know what I hate? I hate Twitter. I think these guys are young guys, and

I think, *Tweet this, Spacebook that.* Whatever. We don't have any hatred for Iowa. We respect Iowa. We have a tremendous amount of respect for their football program and for how they play the game, for how they're coached…. I think that's just young guys tweeting this, twitting that, and that's how it works, I guess."

O'Brien may not care for the unpredictability or unflattering diatribes of the new, modern-day communication outlets favored by the younger generation, but the animosity some of the players and many fans have toward Iowa football is genuine. Since squeezing out a 26–23 double-overtime upset at Beaver Stadium in 2000, Iowa has won eight of the last 10 games. That includes the bitter 24–23 upset in the last minute of the game at Iowa in mid-November 2008 that prevented the then-undefeated No. 2–ranked Penn State team from playing in the BCS National Championship Game. The Lions beat the Hawkeyes 13–3 last season at Beaver Stadium, but what the fans and the veterans of last year's game and the two other defeats since 2008 now want is payback—revenge, right in front of the Hawkeyes' own 70,585 hostile fans in their own revered Niles Kinnick Stadium.

Saturday, October 20, 2012

Kinnick Stadium was electrified as the 7:00 PM CDT kickoff approached. The Big Ten Network cameras panned the grandstand, where a noisy sellout crowd was dressed in alternate sections in their famous black and gold school colors for what had been highly promoted as Black and Gold Spirit Night.

Tonight was a nice Midwest evening with 50-degree temperatures and clouds in the sky. Like Penn State, Iowa was 2–0 in conference games and 4–2 for the season coming into this game but had been beaten in two home games, by intrastate archrival Iowa State, 9–6, and Central Michigan, 32–31. Still, the Hawkeyes' home-field advantage made them a three-point favorite, and beat reporters for both teams predicted a close game, most giving the edge to the team they cover.

A number of screaming Hawkeyes fans sitting close behind the Penn State bench taunted the team and some of their followers sitting nearby before the kickoff. This is just what some of the more antagonistic Iowa fans always do to try and intimidate visiting teams and their fans.

Penn State kicked off after winning the coin toss and deferring, and the fired-up Iowa fans cheered as the Hawkeyes prepared to receive the ball. That was Iowa's last celebration tonight. It was three-and-out in the first three possessions of the game, and the fans of both teams anticipated another of those close, low-scoring defensive games these teams usually have played since Penn State last won in Kinnick Stadium in 1999, 31–7.

With just 4:56 gone in the first quarter, the Lions' NASCAR offense quickly drove from the PSU 16-yard line for a 31-yard touchdown on a pass from McGloin to a wide-open Robinson. About two minutes later, Iowa missed a 49-yard field-goal attempt, and the NASCAR attack went 69 yards for another touchdown reception by Robinson, this one of eight yards. Ficken's second PAT made the score 14–0. Less than four minutes into the second quarter, Iowa missed a 37-yard field goal, and from that point the Hawkeyes did not get past the Lions 45-yard line until the game was almost out of reach at 31–0, with six minutes left in the third quarter.

By the end of the half, Penn State was ahead 24–0 on a 34-yard Ficken field goal and an 11-yard touchdown by Belton set up by a fumble recovered by junior defensive tackle DaQuan Jones at the Iowa 14-yard line. The belligerent Iowa crowd was steaming. They booed as their team left the field and again when the Hawkeyes came out for the second half.

It became worse for all of them in the opening minute of the third quarter. Jesse Della Valle just missed a touchdown on the kickoff return when Iowa's kicker made a shoestring tackle at the Iowa 45-yard line, but McGloin quickly hit redshirt junior wide receiver Brandon Moseby-Felder on a 42-yard pass, and Belton scored from the 3. On Iowa's first play after the kickoff, Mauti intercepted a pass and returned it 20 yards to the Iowa 14, but Zwinak fumbled into the end zone five plays later. A 97-yard drive of nearly seven minutes put the game out of reach in the first minute of the fourth quarter, 38–0, but the Hawkeyes finally scored with a 92-yard kickoff return, and again, with the stadium emptying out and about four minutes remaining, when a 45-yard return of another Zwinak fumble set up an 18-yard touchdown pass.

Final score: 38–14. Statistics of the game: The statistics are again overwhelmingly in Penn State's favor, including time of possession (38:08 to 21:52), red-zone conversions (5-of-6 as compared to 1-of-4) and the rushing (52 carries for 215 yards vs. 23 carries for 20 yards). The Lions easily overcame three major negatives—two lost fumbles, seven penalties for 72 yards, and Iowa's kickoff return for a touchdown.

The Lions players, who had been hugging each other and trading high-fives after almost every touchdown, were jubilant

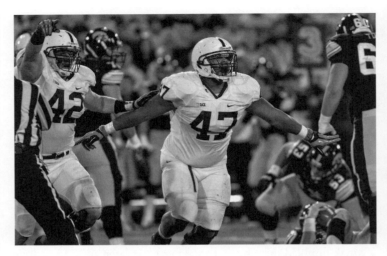

Defensive tackle Jordan Hill (No. 47) and linebacker Michael Mauti (No. 42) celebrate after helping stop Iowa with a fourth-down tackle in Penn State's vengeful 38–14 thumping of the Hawkeyes before their own embarrassed fans. Photo courtesy of Mark Selders, Penn State University Intercollegiate Athletic Archives

as they headed into Iowa's famous pink locker room to continue celebrating.

"It's not always pretty, but I couldn't be happier for the guys in that locker room with the effort in which they played," O'Brien told the media. "They know, at the end of the day, there's only five games left. Through three quarters, I think the [team] did what we wanted them to do. They got a little sloppy in the fourth quarter. They need to learn about playing for 60 minutes." Asked why he used the NASCAR offense most of the game, O'Brien said, "I didn't think we could come in here and just huddle and break the huddle and run a normal pace."

McGloin said the team practiced the no-huddle offense more during the bye week and added new twists just for Iowa. "It's hard to prepare for," he said. "That's a good defense we played today, but I don't think they were ready for it. They couldn't match up with us today, and we were in a lot better shape than them. We got up pretty early, and [their fans] kind of started to die out there. That was one of our main objectives."

Belton, who led the team in rushing with a career day of 103 yards on 16 carries, tried to do his part to silence the crowd after his first touchdown with 5:53 left in the second quarter that gave Penn State a 24–0 lead. He placed his finger to his lips as if to tell the crowd to "shhh" and was hit with a 15-yard penalty for unsportsmanlike conduct. "I kind of got too carried away with it. I got an earful from Coach O'Brien, and I'll never do it again," Belton said.

And all the players were happy to get their revenge on Iowa. As Hill said, "We haven't won here since I was in the second grade."

"To win like that gives us a lot of confidence," Mauti says. "We just have to move on to our next challenge."

What is most satisfying to Penn State fans is the knowledge that Iowa's impertinent and sometimes malicious fans were humiliated today by the thrashing of their team. Everyone who watched knows that, if not for the Nittany Lions' two fumbles and a couple of special teams breakdowns, the final score could have been 50–0 or better.

What this game means to all of the Penn State fans inside Kinnick Stadium and watching on TV is this: Revenge is sweet. Thank you, Bill O'Brien and your special, unforgettable 2012 team.

Chapter 12

Sometimes You Eat the Bear, Sometimes the Bear Eats You

Monday, October 22, 2012

Students began camping out at Nittanyville Monday evening in anticipation of what was expected to be the biggest game of the year against undefeated Ohio State. Before the encampment broke down early Saturday morning, more than 1,200 students in at least 140 groups were there, breaking the record of 111 camping units for the Notre Dame game in 2007.

With both teams banned from the postseason, the only night game this season at Beaver Stadium is already being hyped as "the Ineligible Bowl." It also has been declared an official White House. The Buckeyes are ranked No. 9 in the AP Top 25 poll, and for the first time all season Penn State has received votes. Those 18 votes place them at No. 31, right behind Nebraska and three spots away from Wisconsin—two future opponents.

Tuesday, October 23, 2012

Everyone at O'Brien's weekly press conference was anxious to know how the coach was feeling going into the Ohio State game the following Saturday.

The third person to ask a question at today's weekly O'Brien news conference, Derek Levarse of the *Wilkes-Barre Times-Leader*, asked the coach if he had seen the size of Nittanyville. "There's more kids there now [than there were for Northwestern]," O'Brien responded. "It's unbelievable…. One of the reasons why it's a special place is because of the support of the student body. It gives our players a ton of energy."

Later, in responding to an earlier comment by Ohio State coach Urban Meyer that Beaver Stadium is "the loudest stadium in the Big Ten," O'Brien said, "This is without a doubt the best college football environment in the country…watching that student body [in the previous home games] and listening to our fans and knowing that there's 108,000 people going to be here Saturday night…. This place is going to be loud…everybody's going to be wearing white…. And our team just really wants them to show up early…. It really gets our guys jazzed up in there when they're in there for warm-ups."

O'Brien called Ohio State "probably the best team in the Big Ten…[and] the most talented team we've played to this point in the season…and we're just going to do the best we can in practice this week and try to make sure that we play a good game on Saturday night."

Wednesday, October 24 and Thursday, October 25, 2012

O'Brien and more than 20 players visited the 1,200 tenters at Nittanyville on this night. The following evening O'Brien bought pizzas for dozens of the campers who showed up for his weekly radio call-in program.

Friday, October 26, 2012

A large crowd jammed Recreation Hall for the first Rally in the Valley pep rally in O'Brien's tenure. This continued an annual tradition for these Friday-night pep rallies inside the roughly 6,800-seat indoor sports arena that began in 2005 before another Ohio State game.

Saturday, October 27, 2012

With the tailgate lots open almost 12 hours before the scheduled 6:05 PM kickoff, Penn State fans had a long time to party in the sunny but cool weather.

Today was a battle for the lead in the Big Ten's Leaders Division. Ohio State was originally favored by three points, but by kickoff it was a "pick 'em" game. The game, televised by ESPN, was a sellout, and most of the Penn State fans were in their seats for the warm-up drills, just as O'Brien requested on Tuesday. With the blazing artificial lighting reflecting the White House and the fans yelling, the atmosphere was electric, and the significance of this game to O'Brien and his seniors was apparent when game captains Hill, Hodges, Mauti, McGloin, and Stankiewitch walked to the middle of the field for the coin toss with all the other seniors behind them.

Penn State won the toss, deferred, and Ficken's kickoff went for a touchback. The game immediately turned into a battle for field position and the teams traded four punts until early in the second quarter. The Lions drove 62 yards, primarily on two passes from McGloin to Robinson, but turned over the ball at the OSU 25-yard line after an eight-yard pass attempt on a fourth-and-12 fell four yards short. But one minute and 10 seconds later, backup linebacker Mike Hull blocked the Buckeyes punt at the 14-yard line and Yanich recovered in the end zone. With Ficken's PAT, Penn State led 7–0. The defense again forced a punt with 4:08 left, but a controversial 10-yard holding penalty called on a Lions player in the middle of the line of scrimmage changed the momentum of the game. The Buckeyes used the break to go on to tie the game with a touchdown on third-and-goal at the 1-yard line and the extra point with 0:34 on the clock.

A little more than a minute into the second half McGloin threw just his third interception of the season with a third-and-13 at the Penn State 8-yard line, and the OSU touchdown and PAT gave the Buckeyes a 14–7 lead. Penn State quickly stormed back to OSU's 4-yard line, but after a 10-yard holding penalty on second down, the Lions had to settle for a 27-yard field goal on a fourth-and-goal at the 9-yard line. Following the ensuing kickoff, Braxton threw his only interception of the day at the OSU 44-yard line, but the Buckeyes held, and on fourth-and-9, O'Brien called a fake punt. Butterworth, who had been punting well, rolled out and had his pass attempt to Day batted down. Ohio State drove directly for a touchdown, and that seemed to deflate the Penn State team as well as their fans. The Lions did not get another score until two fourth-quarter touchdowns, one with less than 10 minutes left in the game, with Ohio State leading 28–10, and another with only 1:41 remaining, which made the final score look closer than the game was.

Final score: 35–23. Statistics of the game: Ohio State's sophomore quarterback Braxton Miller's running (25 carries for 134 yards and two touchdowns) vs. Penn State's inefficient running (32 net yards on 28 carries, including 37 yards lost on four sacks), plus the Lions' 5-of-17 third-down conversions and nine penalties for 85 yards.

O'Brien, as usual, primarily blamed himself for the loss, telling media after today's game: "It starts with me. I didn't do a very good job tonight as the head football coach…. We made mistakes, but we win as a team and we lose as a team…. We did some uncharacteristic things tonight…. I could have adjusted better. I could have had a better game plan. We had some line-of-scrimmage penalties that hurt us, jumping offsides and things like that, where we were moving the ball but stalled the drive…. We have to give a lot of credit to Ohio State [for stopping our running game]…. We have to watch the tape and find ways to improve."

O'Brien defended the fake punt, saying, "I just felt like, at that point in time, I wanted to get something going there. We had it. We just didn't execute it." O'Brien wouldn't talk about the controversial holding call on another punt and his animated discussion with the officials protesting the penalty in what some reporters thought was the turning point of the game.

ESPN analyst Chris Spielman, a onetime Ohio State All-American linebacker, called the holding penalty bogus, and some in the media think either the penalty or the botched fake punt was the turning point of the game.

"It's not a letdown," said Morris, who is becoming one of the team's most quotable players. "We have a lot of sane leaders on this team, and we just want to keep moving forward. We have a good record still, 5–3…. We still have the same goal to win our division…. We can't let it affect the rest of our season." Hodges agreed, "It was tough [in the locker room], but we're ready to bounce back next week, and now our goal is 9–3."

So 107,818 people—the largest announced crowd at Beaver Stadium since last year's emotional Nebraska game and the second-largest in two and a half years—went home wondering if they'd just seen the beginning of the end for this emotionally taut team.

Tuesday, October 30 and Wednesday, October 31, 2012

O'Brien's weekly news conference was delayed until Wednesday by Hurricane Sandy, but he did speak to reporters Tuesday as part of the Big Ten coaches' teleconference. At both sessions he responded to questions concerning the morale of his team and the upcoming Purdue game and declined to discuss specifics about the Ohio State loss, saying, "We've moved on."

O'Brien said, "These guys came back to work yesterday and were ready to go [and]…have put that game behind them, and we all have…. They understand that they have four shots left, and it's been really neat to come to practice this week and watch these guys practice with great effort, with passion, compete against each other. Again, that's all because of our senior class and their leadership…. We're just concentrating on Purdue."

He again said he needs to continue doing a better job of coaching, particularly after halftime, since the team has been outscored 42–3 in the third quarter: "We've got to do a better job of adjusting at halftime and coming out with a better plan for the third quarter…. I try to do as good of a job every day of self-critique in making sure I'm doing the best I can for these players and this university. That's every single day, whether we win or lose…. That will never change."

He called Purdue "a very good, a dangerous team," saying, "They have players on both sides of the ball that are playmakers…. It's a big challenge for us on the road."

Monday, October 29 to Friday, November 2, 2012
Reports from the Purdue media indicated head coach Danny Hope could be fired before the end of the season.

Since Hope's hiring in 2008, Purdue's only winning season was 2011, when it went 7–6, but after losing only to Notre Dame, 20-17, in its first four games this year, Purdue has dropped four straight, including blowout losses at home to Michigan and Wisconsin and an embarrassing 44–28 beating at Minnesota last Saturday.

Hope still has four more years left on his contract, but on Monday Purdue's athletics director declined to officially support him. Hope told reporters, "There's still a lot to play for…. I don't believe our team has given up."

Saturday, November 3, 2012
Danny Hope's season became worse and Bill O'Brien's improved as three-and-a-half-point favorite Penn State crushed Purdue 34–9 on a wet, 38-degree late afternoon before an announced crowd of 40,098 and an ESPNU television audience.

What a relaxing game today for the fans! The Lions won the coin toss and deferred. Purdue returned the kickoff 47 yards, and three plays later a 37-yard run gave the home team a first-and-goal at the Penn State 4-yard line. But after a short gain and two incomplete passes, Purdue settled for a 21-yard field goal. This marked the first time a team has scored on Penn State in the first quarter all season. However, the Boilermakers moved past the Lions 40-yard line just once more until midway in the fourth quarter, by which time the game was out of reach at 34–3, when Purdue scored their final points on a two-yard touchdown pass on the last play of the game.

For the first time in his career, Zordich scored two touchdowns in a game, and his six- and five-yard runs capping drives of 48 and 55 yards, respectively, helped give Penn State a 20–3 lead at the intermission. Touchdown passes of 12 and 41 yards on Penn State's first two possessions of the second half climaxed NASCAR drives of 80 and 75 yards and sent thousands of Purdue fans who had not left with their peers at halftime heading for the exits.

Final score: 34–10. Statistics of the game: Penn State's red-zone scoring (5-of-5 vs. 2-for-4), net yards rushing (185 to 87), and passing (321 to 228).

McGloin broke two school records set by All-American Kerry Collins in 1994—throwing for 200 yards or more in seven straight games and passing for 300-plus yards in five games in one season. Zwinak, who beat out Belton for the starting tailback position during the week of practice, also had another career-high game with 134 yards on 21 carries.

Ficken was 2-for-2 on field goals, 4-for-4 on PATs, and had seven kickoffs averaging 62.7 yards. He is now 5-for-12 in field goals after his 2–8 start. His slump is over. Ficken was also among the happiest players in the locker room. He is from Valparaiso, Indiana, about an hour north of Lafayette, and punter Butterworth hails from nearby Indianapolis. Their families hosted large tailgate parties outside the stadium. Ficken told Cory Giger of the *Altoona Mirror* he had 27 tickets for the game and had to borrow some from his teammates: "Having family members in the stadium and my brother and friends here, it felt good to finally have a complete game. Obviously I'm in the groove, and I'm staying confident and building on that."

This was the second-smallest crowd of Nittany Lions fans for an away game, with just 981 getting their tickets through Penn State, including Carole and me. What caught everyone's attention were the attire and pregame antics of strength-and-conditioning coach Craig Fitzgerald. He wore shorts and a T-shirt throughout the cold, damp game, and after a pregame stretch with the team, Fitzgerald tore off his shirt and took a short bare-chested dive, landing chest-first, and the players went wild.

Tuesday, November 5, 2012

Another report from the weekly press conference.

After 10 weeks, O'Brien's weekly news conference continues to be filled with questions about specific players, but today there were more questions about Nebraska and none about the psyche of the team. O'Brien said the starting tailback will continue to be the player who has the best week of practice: "That's really what we try to do at every position," and everyone knows "they have to earn it every day on the practice field…[even] Hodges, Mauti, and Carson." He said Zwinak "has done a really good job for us for the most part, he's a tough kid, he's big, he breaks tackles, he can catch the ball well, he's smart," but he still has to compete with Belton, Zordich, Day, and Dukes.

O'Brien said, "[Nebraska is] an explosive football team that's very well coached…. I would expect that this atmosphere will be very loud, very intense…. They do a great job with their up-tempo, no-huddle package…they have really good fourth quarters. It's going to be a huge challenge for us…to keep it close so in the fourth quarter it's still a game."

Saturday, November 10, 2012

With just a 36–30 loss at UCLA and a 63–38 defeat at Ohio State, No. 16/18 Nebraska was a seven- to eight-and-a-half-point favorite for the 2:30 PM CDT ESPN2/ABC-televised game on an abnormally warm and sunny but windy 76-degree afternoon in Lincoln.

Nebraska won the toss, deferred, and kicked off. Della Valle took the ball on the goal line and returned to the PSU 26-yard line. On third-and-9, McGloin hit Moseby-Felder for a 23-yard gain to the 50-yard line. On the next play, Zwinak went up the middle and ran for a touchdown, and the roughly 2,370 Penn State fans in the sellout crowd of 85,527 stood and cheered.

Nebraska's first score took a little longer. The Huskers drove 65 yards for a first-and-goal at the Penn State 6 but had to settle for a 32-yard field goal. The Lions came right back, going 75 yards to the Nebraska 5-yard line, but Zwinak fumbled and Nebraska recovered at the 6-yard line. This time the Huskers reached Penn State's 10-yard line before kicking a 27-yard field goal 2:31 into the second quarter. But the rest of the half belonged to Lions. A fumbled punt at the Nebraska 31-yard line led to a 10-yard touchdown pass to true freshman tight end Jesse James with 2:42 left in the quarter, and following a short punt by Nebraska and a controversial penalty against Penn State for sideline interference, the Lions drove 35 yards for a 38-yard field goal by Ficken to give Penn State a 20–6 lead.

Nebraska jumped ahead 27–20 with 11 minutes left in the game. Penn State quickly marched 74 yards for a second-and-goal at the Nebraska 3-yard line and seemed to get a touchdown on a pass from McGloin to Lehman near the goal line. But Lehman was

This exclusive photo by Joe Hermitt clearly shows Matt Lehman with the ball over the goal line before his fumble, but the officials on the field and in the replay booth denied Penn State a touchdown in what was a crucial and controversial play in the Lions' bitter 32–23 loss at Nebraska. Photo courtesy of Joe Hermitt, *(Harrisburg) Patriot-News*

hit and fumbled, and Nebraska recovered in the end zone. Although the ABC cameras clearly showed the ball past the goal line before the fumble, the referee did not signal a touchdown and the replay officials did not overturn the call. The Lions forced another punt, and it was a killer of 69 yards to the PSU 2-yard line. On second-and-8, another questionable penalty—for intentional grounding in the end zone by McGloin—gave the Huskers a safety, making the score 29–23. Penn State gained possession at its own 20 with 3:44 left in the game, but on fourth-and-5 at the 25, McGloin's pass attempt failed, and moments later Nebraska kicked a 33-yard field goal to seal the victory.

Final score: 32–23. Statistics of the game: Nebraska's time of possession, for Nebraska (34:19 to 25:41) with a big advantage in the second half (9:58 to 5:02 in the third quarter and 9:00 to 6:00 in the fourth) and red zone advantage with both teams scoring three times on field goals but Nebraska getting three touchdowns on seven times inside the 20-yard line and Penn State just scoring one on six red-zone possessions.

The official statistics didn't show the most significant four plays of the game: Penn State fumbling away the ball twice—although the last one in the fourth quarter included a controversial video replay—and two questionable penalties. True to form, Nebraska made the halftime adjustments and owned the fourth quarter. The Nebraska fans continue to be the most gracious and friendly in major college football, and many of them clapped or shouted encouraging words to the Penn State players as they trudged slowly to the locker room.

The first few questions in O'Brien's six-and-a-half-minute post-game meeting with the media were about fumbles, especially the Lehman fumble and the replay officials' decision not to overturn the call on the field. He said he was told "there was not enough evidence to reverse it…. Matt was trying to reach it out [over the goal line], and he's just trying to make a play." So was Zwinak when he fumbled, O'Brien said: "Twisting, trying to gain extra yards…these are good kids…[but] at end of the day you have to come away with points…. You can't turn the ball over inside the opponent's 10-yard line."

O'Brien's players generally agreed with him on the fumbles and officiating.

"You can't leave the game in the referees' hands," Morris said. "We all know that. They're not perfect. That's just on us, man."

Mauti said, "We shouldn't be in that [replay] position in the first place. We got to hang onto the football when we get in the red zone. We have to do a better job as a defense stopping the run."

We in the television audience not only saw the replay several times but heard the broadcast crew of Sean McDonough and Chris Spielman repeat at least three times during the telecast that Penn State had a touchdown. We also learned what the Fox network's rules analyst, Mike Pereira, the former NFL vice president of officiating, tweeted after the game: "It's a close call in PSU/NEB but if it was me I would have reversed it to a touchdown."

As for the sideline penalty, it had no bearing on the outcome of the game. But it was an extremely rare penalty and is usually only called after a head coach has been warned, because players and coaches consistently clog up along the sideline stripes in front of their bench. When asked about it after the game, O'Brien said he had never been in a game where a sideline penalty was called, but he was told "the referee was running down the sideline and ran into one of our players."

The intentional grounding in the end zone was strictly a judgment call, with the referee, John O'Neill, feeling McGloin was still in the pocket when he threw the ball away. A postgame frame-by-frame analysis of the play showed McGloin was outside the legal pocket. Officials do make misjudgments. But such calls at crucial times in a game make fans wonder if there is something else going on.

What made the crucial intentional grounding penalty and the Lehman replay decision so significant in this game was the opponent. There has been bad blood between Nebraska and Penn State since the early 1980s, stemming from a controversial officiating call in the last minute of Penn State's come-from-behind 27–24 victory at Beaver Stadium in 1982 that helped the Lions win their first national championship. A sideline pass reception at the 2-yard line by tight end Mike McCluskey with 13 seconds left that set up the winning touchdown was ruled in bounds, and although replays were not used by officials at the time and video equipment was not as sophisticated as today, video later showed McCluskey was out of bounds. To this day Nebraska fans believe they were cheated out of a possible national championship. Twelve years later, when voters in the media and coaches' final polls denied Penn State's undefeated 1994 Big Ten and Rose Bowl champions a share of the mythical national title with Nebraska, the Nittany Nation felt that was a makeup call by the pollsters, who were sympathetic to Nebraska's complaint in 1982.

The two events turned what was an occasional matchup between two high-profile college football teams into a highly competitive sports rivalry and one that will only intensify now that both schools are in the same conference.

No doubt this defeat is tougher for Penn State players and their loyal fans to take than the other three. The Huskers congratulated themselves for playing better in the second half and winning the fourth quarter, and the Nittany Lions grumbled about mistakes, fumbles, and penalties. In the end, it all came down to a famous line by a legendary major league spitball pitcher from 1938 to 1954 named Preacher Roe. When he was removed in the second inning of some long-ago game, he said, "Sometimes you eat the bear, sometimes the bear eats you."

Chapter 13

Completed Mission

Monday, November 12, 2012

Penn State was an 18-point favorite over Indiana.

Indiana has never beaten Penn State in the 15 times they've played, starting in Penn State's first year in the Big Ten in 1993. This Hoosiers team is 4–6 for the season, with two wins against Football Championship Subdivision opponents to start the season followed by five straight defeats, including a 31–30 loss to Navy. Then the Hoosiers upset Illinois 31–17 and Iowa 24–21 but lost badly at home last Saturday to Wisconsin, 62–14. With the university's 40,000-plus students starting their Thanksgiving vacation one day before the game, the potential bad weather, and the inferior quality of the opponent, this potentially could be the smallest crowd of the season.

Tuesday, November 13, 2012

Rumors had started to swirl that Bill O'Brien was being interviewed by NFL teams.

At his weekly news conference, O'Brien was asked as many questions (two) about Indiana as about rumors the NFL may lure him back as a head coach.

"Indiana concerns me," he said. "They're a good football team. Offensively they run a very, very fast tempo, I mean ultra-fast, and they try and run between 90 and 100 plays in a game, so that's a huge challenge for our defense this week, and [for] special teams."

O'Brien sidestepped the questions about being mentioned for NFL coaching vacancies, simply saying simply he is "flattered."

O'Brien was asked about the aftereffects of the loss to Nebraska compared to Ohio State and his halftime adjustments in both games, since both opponents took the game away from Penn State after the intermission. He replied: "We can do better things coaching, I'm sure.... We've moved the ball in those games but just haven't scored or maybe turned it over.... Over the next two weeks we need to make sure we do a better job of coming out after halftime.... At the end of the day, sometimes those adjustments work and sometimes they don't.... I wouldn't make too much out of the second-half thing."

A reporter for the *Daily Collegian* told O'Brien he knows a lot of students who are going home for the Thanksgiving break and he wondered if O'Brien is going to do anything to get the students to stay for the Indiana game and return for the finale against Wisconsin. "I'm not going to beg anybody to come to the game," he replied, "but I'm going to tell them this: This is a team that has been through unprecedented situations. This is a football team led by a senior class that has had the choice whether to stay at Penn State or to leave Penn State, and they chose to stay. So as fans, as students, can we not choose to support them in their last two games, eight quarters of football?… This is a team that's poured its heart and soul into this season. We're not an undefeated team, can't do anything about that now…. I would hope and I would expect that our students and our fans understand what this team has been through and what they did to commit to each other, to commit to this university, to stay together and come support them in their last two games, especially this senior class."

Thursday, November 15, 2012

Freezing temperatures and students leaving early for the Thanksgiving break turned Nittanyville into a quiet, downsized campground during the day and a ghost town at night. By rule, when nighttime temperatures are below freezing, tents are permitted only on Thursday and Friday between 8:00 AM and 8:00 PM, and the tents must be removed each night. Campus dormitories remained open until Sunday morning for students planning to attend Saturday's game.

An hour before Thursday's closing, several football players showed up with strength coach Fitzgerald for the Uplifting Athletes Push-Up Challenge for charity. Ten teams of campers competed in a contest of 7,000 push-ups for prizes, including $300 to the winning team, and the football team provided pizzas for all the campers.

Saturday, November, 17, 2012

The day was sunny, with temperatures around 50 for the noon kickoff televised by the Big Ten Network. This game saw a serious injury to Michael Mauti. He already had ACL injuries on both knees that needed surgery and required nearly a year of rehabilitation—the most recent of which had sidelined him for the last 10 games of the 2011 season—and he knew instinctively that his five-year Penn State career was over. "I knew instantly," Mauti told me a few months later. "You don't forget a feeling like that. I didn't want to believe it, but I knew."

Once again the opponents won the coin toss. Indiana chose to receive, and the teams traded punts before IU began a drive that led to one of the worst things that could happen to the 2012 team and a specific player this late in the season.

With the scoreboard clock reading 8:38 remaining in first quarter of a scoreless game, Indiana had a second-and-10 on the Penn State 34-yard line. Tailback Isaiah Roundtree ran up the middle with left guard Collin Rahrig trying to block Michael Mauti. As Mauti fought off Rahrig, another running back, D'Angelo Roberts, came in from Mauti's left and went down low, hitting Mauti just above his left knee. As Mauti moved forward, blocking up the hole, his knee buckled with Rahrig on top, and they went down in a pile with Roundtree, Hill, and Faganano. For a few seconds no one noticed. As Indiana hustled to the scrimmage line for another play, Mauti was on his hands and knees in obvious pain and the team's doctor, Wayne Sebastianelli, and trainer, Tim Bream, rushed on to the field.

Before the cart came out to take Mauti to the Penn State locker room, the entire team ran out to console him: "One Team!" Their inspirational leader, whose outstanding play on the field backed up his fiery and candid words off it, would not be returning to the Beaver Stadium turf today—or ever again—to help the team complete the mission.

I was watching the play develop through my binoculars. Penn State was defending the south end zone where the tunnel is located, so everything was directly in front of me. I remember following the Indiana runner and then seeing Mauti go down with his left leg under his body, and in the seconds that followed it was obvious to me that Mauti knew he had just suffered another ACL injury. I was also listening to Steve Jones and Jack Ham on the radio. From them I learned Mauti was the victim of a dangerous and illegal chop block, but the officials apparently didn't see it, and no penalty was called.

As the cart headed toward the tunnel, I could see Zordich run over and say something to Mauti. No one on the team is closer to Mauti, and you just knew that except for Mauti's family, no one felt worse about what had just happened than Zordich.

After being examined in the locker room, Mauti rejoined his teammates for the fourth quarter wearing a sweat suit and using crutches, and despite his lack of mobility, he was still their leader and kept shouting encouraging words.

At this point of the game, the atmosphere inside the stadium seemed to change—not only with the players but with the spectators—and it was not because of the weather.

Two plays after Mauti left the field, Penn State got the ball at their own 9-yard line following a punt and went 91 yards for a 26-yard touchdown pass to Robinson on a fourth-and-3. Ficken's PAT made it 7–0 with 4:26 left in the quarter.

For nearly the next 30 minutes of the game, Penn State looked a little listless, perhaps still overwhelmed mentally by the upsetting injury to Mauti, while Indiana played like anything but an 18-point underdog.

The second quarter turned into a scoring spree. Indiana shocked Penn State in the first two minutes of the second quarter. A quick 26-yard field goal put Indiana on the board, and moments later an intercepted pass that went through Lehman's hands led to a two-yard touchdown that spurted the Hoosiers to a 10–7 lead. After swapping punts again, McGloin found Robinson on a third-and-4 swing pass, and he dashed for a 53-yard touchdown that is so far the longest play from scrimmage of the season. Indiana hit a 44-yard field goal on their ensuing possession, but Penn State scored two touchdowns in the last seven minutes of the half on drives of 77 and 62 yards and touchdown passes of 10 yards to Robinson and 16 yards to Zwinak, plus Ficken's PATs, to go ahead 28–13 at the intermission.

In the first four and a half minutes of the second half, the stubborn Hoosiers stunned the Lions again by narrowing the lead to 28–22 on a 79-yard touchdown pass and turning a Zwinak midfield fumble into a 46-yard field goal. That woke up the Lions. In the eight and a half minutes before the third quarter ended, they drove 75 and 52 yards for short touchdown runs by Zwinak and Zordich. They added a 28-yard Ficken field goal late in the fourth quarter and then stopped the Hoosiers with a goal-line stand in the last minute of the game to beat the point spread.

Final score: 45–22. Statistics of the game: Penn State's passing (22 receptions for 395 net yards and four touchdowns), rushing offense and defense (44 carries for 151 yards vs. 26 carries for 24 yards), and red-zone success (four touchdowns and a field goal in five attempts).

McGloin continued to surprise the fans who have been critical of him in the past three years by setting or closing in on several school passing records, including new marks for career passing touchdowns (45), single-season completions (251), and single-season yardage (3,071), with his career day of 22-of-32 passes and one interception for 395 yards and four touchdowns.

Robinson's 10 receptions set a new single-season record of 64 to break the mark held jointly by first-team All-Americans O.J.

McDuffie and Bobby Engram, and his three touchdowns put him within two of Engram's single-season record of 66. On defense Hodges emerged from the shadow of the absent Mauti and led the team in tackles with 12, and his interception in the last minute of the first half led to Penn State's fourth touchdown.

Mauti and his parents joined O'Brien and the team to sing the alma mater with the students, and the family's anguish showed on their faces. When they had finished, Hodges went over to the family and hugged them. The players took their turns ringing the victory bell but this time the clang of the bell didn't sound the same without Mauti in uniform.

The first five questions in O'Brien's postgame news conference were about Mauti. O'Brien said he won't know "the diagnosis" for Mauti's knee until next week and that he couldn't say if it was a dirty play that injured him because he had not seen a replay or talked to his assistant coaches. "I've been fortunate to be around some special players," O'Brien said of Mauti. "I've coached a Hall of Fame quarterback, Hall of Fame receivers, great players, and he's one of the most special players I've been around. Like I said from the day I got here, it's about that whole senior class. There's a bunch of special players in that class. He embodies, in my opinion, what Penn State's all about. He's just a fantastic kid…this team's a bunch of resilient guys. When a guy like that, who's a leader on your football team, goes down in a game, I think it was a good response…. They did what they had to do, and I think we got the offense going there around the second quarter."

O'Brien also praised McGloin and credited quarterbacks coach Charlie Fisher with improving McGloin's technique and enhancing his skills, adding in part, "I saw [Matt] become a better leader.

Knowledge is power, so when you know the offense and you know what to do and what everyone else is doing, you have a chance to be a good leader, and I think he's done that this year." He also complimented Robinson: "He is a very unique athlete…and it's a nice combination with him and Matt." O'Brien was also asked about Zwinak's continued fumbling and said Zwinak "is a heck of a player" but that "he has to get better."

O'Brien said he "cannot say enough about our fans. We have great fans…and this team really appreciates it…. The fans were really good today, and I hope that they're great next week."

When asked again if he would be coaching Penn State next season he deferred, saying the media "gave legs to a story last week, and there's no story there…. I'm the head coach of Penn State, and I'm looking forward to getting this team ready for Wisconsin."

Reporters also asked the players about Mauti, and they too mentioned Mauti's leadership and their empathy for him because of what happened. Zordich, his best friend, said every player spoke to Mauti in the locker room. He added, "You hate to see anybody get injured—especially a guy like him that's put so much into the program and is a huge, huge reason why we're all here."

Hill said, "Just seeing a leader go down like that is rough. He's one of our close friends, especially the seniors'. It was a shock and a blow to us as a team. But we knew we had to finish it off."

The announced attendance was 90,358, but there were many empty seats. I estimate there were about 65,000 on hand. Even the student section showed pockets of empty space. Still, I and others were pleased to see so many there despite the Thanksgiving break. We were concerned many of these students would go home and not return for the Wisconsin game. We also worried about the kooky late November weather in State College. Although it is usually cold, frequently freezing, and sometimes snowy, there have been years when the temperatures have been in the 50s, like today, and even in the high 60s on couple of occasions.

Mauti's injury put a damper on the postgame tailgating. Many fans left for home or local pubs to watch the Wisconsin–Ohio State game on television. At the start of today, Penn State and Wisconsin were tied for second in the Big Ten Leader's Division with a 4–2 record behind 6–0 Ohio State. A Wisconsin win, coupled with a Michigan victory over Ohio State next Saturday in its traditional end-of-season game could mean a co–division championship for the winner of the Penn State–Wisconsin game. No one in college football would have believed that possible when the NCAA sanctions came down in July. The Navy SEAL Rick Slater was right: "Charlie Mike!" Continue Mission.

Tuesday, November 20, 2012

Of the 21 questions put to O'Brien in his last Tuesday news conference of the season, the only one about Wisconsin was the 19th. Three of the first four and the ninth were about the senior class. In my diary entry for that day, I wrote the highlights of what he said about the seniors of the 2012 season, and these remarks could be their extended epitaph for history.

About the seniors, O'Brien said, "It's hard to put into words what this senior class means to this football program, to this athletic department, and to this university. These are young guys that have been through a lot. They have been through the death of their former head coach, a legendary coach. They have been through the things that went on off the field that don't need to be repeated…. They have hung tough, dealing with the NCAA and the sanctions…. They've been through the fact that they had to lead this football team and keep these guys together. At the age of 21, 22, some of them 23 years old, that's pretty heavy stuff, and you can't say enough about them.

"It's pretty neat to watch these guys handle things, pick themselves up and charge forward and do it the right way. We're not a pretty bunch, we're 7–4; we wish we could have some games back where we thought we could have played better, but we do play hard, and a lot of that has to do with the senior class and buying into a new way of doing things…. They mean a lot to me personally; they mean a lot to our coaching staff. We came in here, we were hired in January, and I didn't show up until after the Super Bowl, so I have not even known these guys a full year, but I remember when we first came here…we did things differently…they bought right in, and our coaching staff had a lot to do with that…. I did make it a priority within the team to make sure that the seniors were put into leadership roles, whether it was each guy [being] a captain this year for a game or leading the stretch lines or breaking it down at the end of practice or a workout…. I will always remember these guys and hopefully be able to have relationships with them for the rest of my life."

O'Brien also urged fans who will be attending Saturday's finale to be in Beaver Stadium a half hour before the scheduled 3:30 kickoff to honor the seniors and their families on the traditional Senior Day. "That's a big deal," he said. "I know that we have honored the seniors in the past, but I don't think we have included their families. That's the least we can do for this senior class, this particular one this year, is honor [the families]. So we need everybody in their seats at 3:00 on Saturday."

Among the other questions during the news conference were three about Mauti. O'Brien said he couldn't comment about the extent of Mauti's injury or the possibility of him applying to the NCAA as a sixth-year medical redshirt. "He won't play against Wisconsin, and that's a tough deal for us and a tougher deal for him," O'Brien said. "He comes from a great family…. I met with him and his parents on Sunday, especially him, and, it's tough for him…. He's a football guy. He loves Penn State and he loves his teammates, so it's a difficult thing for him personally…. Obviously, he's been around us all week, he's in the meetings and he will be at practice today, he will be around [Saturday too]."

O'Brien praised Wisconsin as "a big, tough football team that is going to run" with a "great running back" in Montee Ball and "great tight ends" and a "stout, physical" defense. He said, "We have to be able to [run]. We can't go in there and throw it 60 times…. You always want to win your last game, and it's going to be difficult to do that…. I think we're going to have to do a great job of controlling our emotions, because it's going to be an emotional beginning to that game…. I'm encouraged because we had a really good practice yesterday, and it's a cool week. It's Thanksgiving and you're practicing, and this is what football is all about: Wisconsin versus Penn State. I heard maybe it's going to snow, which would be great."

Wednesday, November 21, 2012

O'Brien made his final appearance of the year at the Quarterback Club and was given a standing ovation.

Earlier in the day, an editorial in the State College–area newspaper the *Centre Daily Times* commented on the reports that O'Brien might leave to take an NFL job and said in part: "O'Brien has brought a calming presence to the squad and has been widely embraced in the community and across the Penn State fan base. He has reached out to support local causes and has been the university's most prominent cheerleader for its academics and its athletics. It will be a sad day for the Nittany Nation when O'Brien leaves, whether that occurs in the coming weeks or many years from now. But one lesson learned through the past 12 months of criminal charges and controversy is that no one person is bigger than Penn State, bigger than the football or athletic programs, bigger than the community. O'Brien has helped lead the chorus of 'One Team' all season, and that slogan has proved true. A superb senior class helped hold the team together in the late summer, when defections and uncertainty could have been devastating…the support of this team from the university, students, alumni and Penn State fans has never wavered. The 'One Team' mantra has extended well beyond the football roster."

Thursday, November 22, 2012

Thanksgiving Day. This was the final practice for the 2012 team and the last practice ever for its 31 seniors.

Today was a sunny, unseasonably warm day with temperatures into the high 50s, and at the end of practice, O'Brien introduced a new tradition. The seniors walked single file through a double line of their teammates and coaches, who clapped and exchanged handshakes or hand slaps with each one. Then they made their way inside Holuba Hall for last words by O'Brien and a final cheer of "One Team."

Later, McGloin and Morris used Twitter to acknowledge the last practice and compliment their teammates: McGloin wrote, "Happy thanksgiving. Last practice at PSU is over. It's been an honor and a blessing to play here. One game left to make it special. #OneTeam." And Morris tweeted, "My last practice in this uniform wit this team & seniors. With my bro @j_hill_47."

Also today, a column in the *New York Times* by one of the most well-respected sportswriters in America, Dave Anderson, singled out the 2012 team as one of his list of 26 teams and individuals "in sports' little corner of the world who quietly deserve a Thanksgiving Day thank-you," referring to them as "The Penn State football players who stayed with Coach Bill O'Brien to produce a 7–4 record, rather than transferring after the Jerry Sandusky scandal."

Friday, November 23, 2012

On Friday, after the team's final walk-through in preparation for Wisconsin, O'Brien gave each senior a chance to speak to the team. Later some of them told Mark Dent of the *Pittsburgh Post-Gazette* what they said:

"Some seniors spoke briefly and some spoke for a long time. Junior offensive guard John Urschel said linebacker Michael Mauti's speech was particularly inspiring.

"Senior cornerback Stephon Morris loved hearing from his classmates. He said Jake Fagnano and Matt McGloin told the stories of how they made it from walk-ons to contributors. He said he didn't expect Gerald Hodges to get emotional, but he did. 'We shared our life,' Morris said. 'Pretty much what Penn State means to us.'

"Among the differing speeches, senior center Matt Stankiewitch noticed a common thread. Every senior thanked O'Brien. 'For building the staff that he did,' Stankiewitch said, 'and building up the Penn State community from the shadows and ashes.'"

Word also leaked out this day that the 2012 team would receive a special historical honor that had been given to only 15 previous Penn State teams since 1887, for winning national championships and conference titles or for being undefeated. The years of those teams are embedded on the façade below the private suites on the east side of Beaver Stadium. On Saturday, the year 2012 would be placed alongside the 2008 team that won the Big Ten championship.

It was later disclosed that the marker was proposed by then–acting athletics director Dave Joyner. "My family and I were talking about what a special team this was," Joyner told me later, "and we needed to do something to honor them. It might have been my son Andy who first suggested it, and we all knew this was the right thing to do. I talked it over with Coach O'Brien and some others in the administration and athletic department, and we did it."

(On January 21, 2013, President Erickson appointed Joyner athletics director for the rest of Erickson's presidential term.)

Saturday, November 24, 2012

Senior Day. Bill O'Brien didn't get the snowstorm he wanted, but it was a cold and blustery day with temperatures of 30 to 34 degrees and winds at 16 to 23 MPH, which made it feel in the 20s, with intermittent snow flurries.

ESPN2 was televising the game, but about 30 minutes before the network went on the air, after both teams finished their warm-ups, Senior Day ceremonies began for the 31 seniors and three senior managers. This one was different from any others in the past.

O'Brien personally greeted each senior player and manager as their names were called by Beaver Stadium public-address announcer Dean DeVore, and they walked out on the field from the tunnel carrying a bouquet of flowers for their mothers or girlfriends, who were waiting at the end of a long double line formed by the rest of 2012 team.

The five team captains who were elected Thursday but not announced until the pregame meal this morning were introduced last—linebacker Mike Yanich for special teams, McGloin and Zordich for the offense, and Hill and Mauti for the defense. Mauti received the loudest cheering and applause from the fans, most of whom were standing. He was walking and jogging, his left leg in a leg brace, and he was dressed for the cold weather, wearing his uniform jersey and a baseball cap.

The underclassmen left for the locker room, and the seniors posed for the traditional group photo. Just as they started jogging toward the tunnel, DeVore's voice over the loudspeakers stopped them. Everyone looked toward the east grandstands below the private suites, at about the 30-yard line, near the student section, and DeVore said:

"To say that this team has represented our athletic program, our great university, and our worldwide alumni in the most noble of ways during the most trying of times proves the rare inadequacy of words. So today we memorialize this team for its profound commitment and contributions to Penn State by ensuring they will be recognized alongside the very greatest teams in our program's history. We are pleased to unveil this year 2012 and add this Penn State Nittany Lion football team to its rightful place in our rich and storied history."

A white banner was removed to reveal the embedded 2012 team marker in bold blue numbers, and the crowd stood and cheered lustily.

It is unfortunate there was not a capacity crowd there to witness this memorable moment saluting the 2012 team. Thousands of seats were empty, and most of them remained unfilled even after the ball was kicked off at 3:35. The student section was less than half full, and it was particularly noticeable in the senior section in the upper east grandstands at the goal line. So much for Kirk Herbstreit's "best student section in the country." This team, especially, deserved better from their classmates.

The seniors rejoined their teammates in the locker room, and when they ran out of the tunnel after the usual pregame activities by the Lions mascot, cheerleaders, and Blue Band, the fans began to notice some players had a blue number on their usually plain white helmets. In looking closer, they saw it was the same number: 42. Later everyone learned Zordich and Hill had asked all the seniors

Penn State fans salute the senior class leadership of the 2012 team with this card stunt declaring "Thank You Seniors" just moments before the kickoff of the final game of the season against Wisconsin on Thanksgiving weekend. Photo courtesy of Steve Manuel

to place Mauti's number on their helmets, and they enthusiastically agreed. It took the crowd a little longer to realize Hodges was also wearing Mauti's number on his jersey too, in a personal salute to his fellow senior linebacker.

Penn State was a two-point favorite, following Wisconsin's 21–14 loss at home to Ohio State last Saturday. Going into the game, the Lions were second and Wisconsin third in the Leaders Division behind Ohio State, which has clinched the division.

In an earlier game that started at noon, Ohio State beat Michigan 26–21, and Nebraska defeated Iowa 13–7. That meant no matter the outcome of today's game, Wisconsin would play Nebraska for the official Big Ten championship and the Rose Bowl.

Four of the five new captains walked hand in hand to midfield for the coin toss. I wondered why special teams captain Mike Yanich was not with the other four captains but on the sideline. I later learned a Big Ten rule permits only four players on each side for the coin toss.

The Lions won the coin flip and deferred, and as the teams took the field before the kickoff, thousands of spectators in the lower section of the east stands displayed a gigantic blue-on-white stunt card that read:

THANK YOU SENIORS

Ficken's kickoff toward the north end was returned 23 yards to the Penn State 26-yard line, and after three running plays that ate up nearly 90 seconds, Wisconsin stunned the Lions and the crowd with a 57-yard pass for a touchdown. It was the first time all season an opponent has been the first to score on Penn State. The Lions struck back on a 15-play, 78-yard drive—with Zwinak carrying nine times for 41 yards—to tie the game on Zwinak's three-yard touchdown and Ficken's PAT. Wisconsin quickly regained the lead at 14–7 with a 47-yard kickoff return and four straight running plays as Montee Ball scored a 17-yard touchdown with 6:27 left in the first quarter.

Wisconsin's special teams and its run-it-down-their-throat offense was doing what no other opponent had done all year in the first quarter, and the fans were nervous. This did not look like the same defense they had been watching all year.

Defensive coordinator Mac McWhorter and his defensive assistants gathered with their players along the bench, and when they came back on the field after Wisconsin forced a punt, nothing seemed to have improved. In seven rushing plays and one pass completion, the Badgers went from their 34-yard line to the Penn State 31, but on a fourth-and-5, they were penalized for illegal procedure and had to punt. Wisconsin did not get that deep into Lions territory again until about five minutes were left in the game.

Although thousands of fans left at halftime because of the frigid weather, Penn State began to change the momentum of the game after the second-half kickoff with long drives of 77 and 72 yards but had to settle for field goals on both. The first drive sputtered after a first-and-goal at the Wisconsin 10 when a third-down six-yard pass to Moseby-Felder, tiptoeing in the back of the end zone for an apparent touchdown, was overturned by the television replay officials who ruled he juggled the ball falling out of bounds. So Ficken kicked a 23-yard field goal.

Two possessions later, the second drive faltered with a fourth-and-3 at the Wisconsin 15, and Ficken booted a 32-yard field goal with three minutes left in the third period. After the defense forced the seventh straight Badgers punt and despite a 15-yard penalty for offensive interference, the Lions finally took a 21–14 lead two minutes into the fourth quarter, after a 67-yard drive. Freshman tight end Jesse James scored the touchdown on a 41-yard pass from McGloin, and Zwinak ran for the two-point conversion.

As snow flurries drifted over the stadium, Wisconsin reached the Penn State 20-yard line after a 59-yard drive with five minutes remaining in the game, before a fourth-and-8 pass attempt was intercepted by Fagano at the 6 and returned 13 yards. However, it was three-and-out for the Lions offense, and after the punt, the Badgers drove 56 yards for a first-and-goal at the Lions 9-yard line with about one minute left in the game.

The Penn State crowd was on its feet screaming "Defense! Defense!" Ball was stopped for no gain, and Wisconsin called timeout. A short pass gained seven yards, but Ball was tackled for a two-yard loss by Hill and Hull, and Wisconsin took its final timeout with 23 seconds left. It became a guessing game for the defense—a run or a pass. The Badgers passed, scoring a four-yard touchdown, and Kyle French tied the game with his third PAT of the day. Overtime!

Wisconsin won the coin toss and chose to be on defense first. Penn State selected to attack the north goal rather than the south goal, which is usually louder because of the students.

Sitting high above the south end zone, I wondered why Penn State had selected to defend the other end zone. Not only is the crowd normally louder in this end zone because of the students, which would help both the Lions offense and defense on this first overtime session, but the south end zone seemed better for Penn State's offense in the blustery weather, with the wind blowing toward us.

McGloin's first-down pass was incomplete. Zwinak gained six yards, but another pass attempt was incomplete, and on fourth down at the Badgers 19-yard line, Ficken kicked a 37-yard field goal just inside the left crossbar.

On Wisconsin's first play, Ball gained only one yard. Then Badgers quarterback Curt Phillips fumbled when sacked by Stanley, but Wisconsin recovered at its 27-yard line. Phillips tried another pass. Linebacker Glenn Carson, subbing at Mauti's position, almost intercepted but could not hold on to the ball. French came on for a 44-yard field-goal attempt. He had made 2-of-4 kicks this season from beyond the 40-yard line, including a 46-yarder against Illinois.

The crowd was on its feet again, screaming. The ball was snapped, and French had the distance as the ball sailed toward the goal posts. But the ball drifted left and missed badly. The crowd erupted even louder than before as the Penn State players on the sideline swarmed onto the field, jumping up and down and hugging each other.

Final score: 24–21 (OT). Statistics of the game: Between Wisconsin's first two possessions and its last two before overtime, the Badgers had a total of 97 net yards on the eight other times with the ball, and the Lions defense held Ball to 111 net yards on 27 carries while Zwinak rushed for 179 net yards on 39 carries for his fourth straight game running for 100 yards or more. Penn State also did not have a turnover, compared to a crucial one for Wisconsin, and finished the season with a 22–13 and 9+ turnover ratio.

I found it apropos that Joe Paterno's historic last game was won by a field-goal kicker and that today's historic game was too, both by players he recruited.

As for overtime, this was Penn State's first overtime victory at home after two losses, giving the Lions a 3–3 overtime record dating back to the 26–23 double-overtime loss to Iowa at Beaver Stadium in 2000.

With many of the remaining fans still watching, the players and coaches stood in front of the student section, arms locked together, swaying side to side jubilantly as a happy Bill O'Brien, with a microphone in his hands, led them in singing the alma mater. Each player rang the victory bell with more enthusiasm than ever before, and then they celebrated in the locker room as if they won a national championship—which, in many symbolic ways, they did. The players all gathered in a circle, yelling and screaming and jumping up and down and then chanting "O-B! O-B! O-B!" several times. Bill O'Brien hurled himself into the middle of the team. When they quieted down, their coach told the players how proud he is of what they have done this season:

"There are really no words to describe what this is like. But it's like what we talked about all week, man. This is the locker room we wanted to be in. And the only thing I've got to say is this: Thank you, seniors. Personally, our coaching staff, and all your teammates, we'll remember you forever. What you meant for this program, what you meant for this university, we'll remember you forever. Just understand that."

When O'Brien was finished, they all raised their hands toward the air in a circular arch and for what O'Brien yelled was "one final time," they cheered "One Team." Then, as O'Brien drifted away to meet with the media, the players yelled "We Are…Penn State!" 10 times.

O'Brien's euphoria carried over into the media room, and once again he effusively praised his seniors: "There was a lot riding on this game for these players.... To think that we won eight of our last 10 games.... It would've been terrible to come in here and not win that game after that pregame ceremony. When they put your 2012 team up there with those other teams...those are undefeated, championship teams. That means a lot."

O'Brien was asked about several players, and he complimented Ficken, Hill, Zwiank, Fagnano, and others, as well as the defensive coaches and players for making great adjustments after Wisconsin's two quick touchdowns in the first quarter. In part, he said, "It's a testament to those kids on defense and that coaching staff over there. They did a nice job all night.... I can't say enough about [Ficken] and the way he rallied tonight and made some big kicks for us.... To think of where he came from to where we are tonight, kicking the winning kick.... It's just hard to put into words what Jordan Hill's meant to this team. He just plays so hard. He's an excellent football player.... He's a phenomenal kid off the field. He's great in the locker room.... And Zach has really played well for us the last six, seven, eight weeks of the season.... [When] you rush for 180 yards against Wisconsin's defense, you're doing something good because Wisconsin's got a very stout defense."

No one was happier than the seniors, and they made sure the reporters knew it. This is a sampling of their postgame comments:

—Hill: "It was a storybook ending. I want this team to go down in history, not for the wins but for the character of all our guys and everything that we've been through and how to overcome stuff when you get knocked down."

—Zordich: "This [game] goes at the top for me. There's just too many emotions that go into this game."

—Morris: "I'm just so happy for this team, for this university, especially my senior class. Won a big game like that and the way we defended together…. The way I went out in my career, I could not have asked for a better ending."

—Fagnano: "This really describes my journey through Penn State. I've been dreaming of playing here my whole life. It's been a tough journey…. Things went my way. Things didn't. The interception just tops everything."

—McGloin: "It's exciting to go down as one of the great teams in Penn State history. To have that season stapled on the stadium forever is a great feeling, and to be a part of it is exciting…. Eight wins is good. I still think we should be a lot better than that, but we finished the season on a high note, and it's the way the seniors wanted to go out."

—Mauti: "I'm tearing up thinking about [Hodges wearing my uniform and the players with my number on their helmets]. It was the biggest honor for me. We have come so far in our relationship and as players…. [This] is such a special thing to be a part of, and I am just proud to be a part of it."

It's a shame there weren't more fans inside Beaver Stadium to watch today's historic day unfold. The announced attendance was 93,505, but that far exceeds the actual number of spectators, and by the time the team was celebrating after Wisconsin's missed field goal, the initial crowd had dissipated substantially. That may have been because of the near-freezing weather. It certainly didn't bother strength-and-conditioning coach Craig Fitzgerald, who was once again wearing only shorts and a T-shirt.

As Carole and I watched the emotions of the seniors and their families in the pregame ceremony and later sang along with Bill O'Brien and all the players singing the alma mater, we couldn't help but get a little emotional ourselves. And we could tell by the fans still around us in the upper deck of the south end zone that many of them felt like we did.

We're simply members of the Nittany Nation. We've been going to Penn State games together since the mid-1950s, and we have been there when they won two national championship games and lost two others. We have watched them in the postseason bowl games when they concluded four of their five undefeated seasons, and we have been in the stadiums when they clinched their three Big Ten titles. Those were great teams, and they all have the numerals of their season on the façade below the private boxes at Beaver Stadium. The 2012 team now has its "rightful place in our rich and storied history."

Later this evening, the players and coaches celebrated with their families at a private party at a State College restaurant, and there was a password used to enter the party. It summed up perfectly the remarkable journey of Penn State's 2012 football team: "Charlie Mike—Completed Mission!"

Chapter 14

Hail to the Lions

Sunday, November 25, 2012

John Feinstein, another of the nation's best-known sportswriters, praised the 2012 team in a *Washington Post* column reflecting on the college football season: "Bill O'Brien and his coaching staff and his players produced one of the most memorable seasons in college football history.... It's easy to play for championships and for glory. It is what most athletes do. It's hard to play when nothing you do can completely erase a horrible stain and when you know there's no championship and very little glory at stake. Penn State's players did that."

Thursday, November 29, 2012

Rick Reilly, one of the most respected and acclaimed sportswriters in America, dating back to his years at *Sports Illustrated*, called O'Brien "Everybody's Coach of the Year" in his ESPN.com column. Reilly was one of the severest critics of Penn State and Joe Paterno in the Sandusky scandal but he had high praise for O'Brien:

"Into the teeth of the worst college football scandal in American history, into a sex-scandal mess the National Guard couldn't have cleaned up, Bill

O'Brien pulled off a football miracle: He made you forget Penn State was radioactive.

"O'Brien went 8–4 in the middle of nuclear winter. He kept popping open umbrellas while it rained bowling balls. He made a numb town feel again. That's why he's either the coach of the year in college football this season or you melt down the trophy."

Saturday, December 1, 2012
Seattle Times sportswriter Dwight Perry proposed a new Comeback Program of the Year Award for Penn State.

Monday, November 26, 2012
Six players were selected to the 2012 All–Big Ten first teams, including Mauti and Robinson, who were named Players of the Year at their positions. Mauti was selected as the Butkus-Fitzgerald Linebacker of the Year and Robinson received the Richter-Howard Receiver of the Year. Hill was chosen as Penn State's recipient of the Sportsmanship Award, given to one player on each conference team.

Both the coaches' and the media polls selected Mauti, Robinson, and Hill on their first teams, while Stankiewitch and Urschel also were selected by the coaches and freshman tight end Carter was selected by the media. Hodges joined Stankiewitch and Urschel on the media's second team and also was placed on the coaches' second team. Seven players earned honorable mentions: McGloin, Morris, Zwinak, Stanley, Farrell, Adrian Amos, and Barnes.

Mauti, Robinson, and Hill were also unanimous choices for the Big Ten Network Team of the Year, with O'Brien named Coach of the Year and Barnes Freshman of the Year while Stankiewitch tied with Wisconsin's Travis Frederick for the center position.

Although McGloin was the Big Ten's leading passer, he was bypassed by both the coaches and the media for their first or second teams. Nebraska's Taylor Martinez was the first-team choice of the coaches, and Ohio State's Braxton Miller was the media selection, with their positions switched for the second teams. McGloin was the only quarterback receiving honorable mention in the coaches' poll, while Michigan's Denard Robinson and Northwestern's Kain Colter joined McGloin as a media honorable mention.

I wonder if McGloin would have made at least one of the second teams, if not a first team, but for his reputation before this season as an erratic, mediocre quarterback who threw too many interceptions. By the time McGloin proved he had become an outstanding quarterback in O'Brien's system, Martinez and Miller had lived up to some of their preseason hype and McGloin couldn't overcome their preseason stature in the minds of the voters.

Tuesday, November 27, 2012

O'Brien was selected the Big Ten Coach of the Year by the coaches and the media, and Barnes was named the conference's Freshman of the Year.

"This is a fantastic honor; it's very humbling," O'Brien said. "Any time you are named Coach of the Year, it has a lot to do with two groups of people—it's your coaching staff and obviously your players."

Thursday, November 29, 2012

Michael Mauti and his family wrote an open letter to the Penn State family and distributed it to multiple news outlets. It read:

"To Nittany Nation/PSU community,

"Wow! We are not sure where to begin. The outpouring of support that we have received has been truly humbling and moving in more ways you can imagine. We could not be more touched and honored to be included in this incredibly unique community. Saturday was truly special for our entire family and for all the seniors and their families that know what the words commitment, family, community, and leadership really mean. We will remember that day for the rest of our lives. I don't think the phrase 'thank you' does enough justice but from our family to the entire PSU community...THANK YOU from every emotional fiber in our hearts!!!

"WE ARE...

"As 'Proud' as ever!!!

"The Mauti Family"

Monday, December 3, 2012

McGloin won the Burlsworth Trophy as the walk-on of the year in college football.

O'Brien was one of nine finalists for the 2012 Eddie Robinson Coach of the Year Award sponsored by the Football Writers Association of America (FWAA). The award was given on January 6, but O'Brien lost out to Brian Kelly of Notre Dame.

Stankiewitch was one of six finalists for the Rimington Trophy, given to the nation's outstanding center. A.Q. Shipley, cocaptain of the 2008 Big Ten championship team, was the only Penn State player who had won the award since it was created in 2000, and he remains as such, because the winner was announced on December 6, and it was not Stankiewitch.

Tuesday, December 4, 2012

O'Brien was a finalist for another Coach of the Year award, this time one sponsored by Liberty Mutual in partnership with the National Football Foundation and College Football Hall of Fame. He again lost to Brian Kelly.

The prestigious Maxwell Club announced the 2012 Penn State football team as the winner of the organization's Thomas Brookshier Spirit Award in recognition of their commitment, leadership, and outstanding effort during the season. In making the announcement, the club's president, Ron Jaworski, said, "The senior leaders at Penn State demonstrated incredible commitment, character, and effort during the past year, and what they accomplished on the field this fall is just astonishing. With the difficult circumstances surrounding the program it would have been easy for many of these players to look for a different situation to finish their college careers. But they chose to stay and support their teammates, coaches, and university. The spirit and courage demonstrated in their actions is worthy of recognition with the Thomas Brookshier Spirit Award. They are a very special group of young men."

The award, named after the deceased onetime star defensive back of the Philadelphia Eagles and also a nationally known sportscaster, was presented at the club's 76th annual awards gala in Atlantic City on March 1.

Also on this day, Hill was selected a second-team All-American by Athlon Sports.

Thursday, December 6, 2012

Pete Massaro and John Urschel were named first-team Academic All-Americans by the College Sports Information Directors of America (CoSIDA). This was a repeat for Massaro, from the 2010 team.

Also, Hodges was selected New Jersey Player of Year for FBS/Division I college football, an award sponsored by the Brooks-Irvine Memorial Football Club of South Jersey.

Penn State's all-time total of 51 Academic All-Americans in football is No. 3 among schools in the Football Bowl Subdivision.

The Nittany Lions also have had the most Academic All-Americans (15) of any school since 2005. That these statistics, coupled with football's consistent graduation rates of 80 percent or more as reported by the NCAA in the last eight years—including 91 percent in the 2012 report covering the four-year period of 2002 to 2005—are among the best in the nation makes a mockery of the so-called "culture of football" claims cited by the NCAA to support its wrongheaded sanctions.

Friday, December 7, 2012

Barnes and Carter were named to the Sporting News, FoxSportsNet.com, and CBSSports.com All-Freshman teams.

Saturday, December 8, 2012

In the late afternoon, the seniors on the 2012 team were honored in a halftime ceremony during the men's basketball game at the Bryce Jordan Center after signing autographs for nearly an hour before the game on the BJC's concourse.

In addition, O'Brien was chosen as national Coach of the Year, and Mauti was selected a first-team All-American by AT&T ESPN, the joint venture that sponsors the ABC/ESPN Play of the Week, with AT&T also the exclusive wireless sponsor of ESPN's telecasts of the BCS.

Sunday, December 9, 2012

A near-record crowd of nearly 1,000 filled the Penn Stater Conference Center Ballroom for the annual Quarterback Club Senior Banquet, featuring the senior awards.

There was a new twist this year. In the past, underclassmen have attended and sat among the attendees, with at least one player at each table. O'Brien changed that, limiting the players at the dinner to seniors only. The rest of the format remained the same.

After the playing of the national anthem, the seniors and their families were introduced individually as they walked into the middle of the banquet room, toward the head table. The crowd applauded politely as each name was called, but the loudest applause came when McGloin, Mauti, and Zordich were introduced. After the meal service, the senior awards were given.

Mauti received the Lions' Pride Outstanding Senior Player. "This is a sad and happy time," he said after the applause had died down. "I've been through a lot, and we've been through a lot." Mauti then told an anecdote about after the team had lost its first two games: "Zordich came to me and said, 'We better win, or we're going to look stupid on TV.'"

This was the best line of the banquet, and the crowd loved it.

Three of the 11 awards were new. Here is a list of the winners, with the newest awards at the end.

—Lions' Pride Outstanding Senior Player: Mauti

—John Bruno Jr. Memorial Award (for outstanding member of special teams): Day and Yancich

—Ridge Riley Award (for sportsmanship, scholarship, leadership, and friendship): Massaro and McGloin

—Richard Maginnis Memorial Award (for outstanding offensive lineman): Farrell and Stankiewitch

—Robert B. Mitinger Jr. Award (for courage, character, and social responsibility): Zordich

—Outstanding Run-On Award (for run-on player who exemplifies total commitment, loyalty, hard work, and courage): Michael Fuhrman and J.R. Refice

—Nittany Lion Club Academic Achievement Award (for highest GPA): McGregor (3.85 GPA)

—Quarterback Club Special Awards: Mark Arcidiacono, Joe Baker, P.J. Byers, Cody Castor, Andree Dupree, Jacob Fagnano, Patrick Flanagan, Frank Figueroa, Brian Irvin, Christian Kuntz, Evan Lewis, James Terry, Jamie Van Fleet, Garrett Venuto, and Mike Wallace

—Coaches' Award (for pride, dedication, commitment, and exemplary leadership in addition to outstanding performance): Hodges and Morris

—Football Letterman's Club Joe and Sue Paterno Post-Graduate Scholarship ($5,000 scholarship to provide recognition and financial assistance for graduate school): Emery Etter

—Reid-Robinson Award (for outstanding defensive lineman named in honor of College Football Hall of Famers Dave Robinson and Mike Reid): Hill and Stanley

Monday, December 10, 2012

Barnes and Carter were named to the Freshman All-American first teams by CollegeFootballNews.com and James was an honorable mention.

In addition, O'Brien was chosen Big Ten Coach of the Year by BTN.com, and four players were named to both All–Big Ten teams selected by ESPN.com and BTN.com: Mauti, Hill, Stankiewitch, and Robinson. Carter was also selected only for the ESPN.com team, while Barnes was chosen only for the BTN.

Friday, December 14, 2012

Mauti was selected a first-team All-American linebacker by *Phil Steele's College Football Preview*.

Sunday, December 16, 2012

O'Brien was named one of six finalists for the Dapper Dan Charities Sportsman of the Year Award that goes to the coach or player that brings the most recognition to western Pennsylvania. Unfortunately he went on to lose to Pittsburgh Pirates outfielder Andrew McCutcheon.

Tuesday, December 18, 2012

The Bear Bryant Coach of the Year Award selected O'Brien as one of six finalists, which also included Ohio State's Meyer, Texas A&M's Kevin Sumlin, Kansas State's Bill Snyder, Stanford's David Shaw, and Vanderbilt's James Franklin. The National Sportscasters and Sportswriters Association vote on the award, which is sponsored by the American Heart Association and Marathon Oil.

Joe Paterno was the recipient of the award in its first year in 1986, and his trophy has been on display in the football wing of the Penn State All-Sports Museum since it opened in February 2002.

Monday, January 7, 2013

In a long opening statement, O'Brien told media during a news conference in Beaver Stadium why he looked at the NFL and why he would be staying at Penn State:

"Out of respect for what we did this year, myself and our staff, and most importantly our players, and plus some of the things that I have done in the past, a few [NFL] teams reached out to my representative, and we had conversations," O'Brien said. "That's as far as it went. At the end of the day, the most important thing is the decision that I made. I made the decision to be here at Penn State, just like I made that decision a year ago, and I can't think of a better place to be. This is a top 10 football program. This is one of the best academic institutions in the country, in the world, and I am very, very proud to be the head football coach here. Very proud."

O'Brien said neither money nor "structural changes" within the athletic department had anything to do with his decision. He also made it clear his ultimate ambition is to be a head coach in the NFL. "Number one is, I'm a coach," he said. " Coaching is something that I love.... I love coaching these kids here at Penn State. I enjoy coming into the office every day and strategizing and thinking about how we can get this team ready for the 2013 season. I enjoy the week-to-week preparation. I enjoy the practice planning, the camaraderie with our staff.... We have a fantastic staff of guys, and I am a coach.... My profession is coaching, and in my profession, the National Football League is the highest level of coaching...again, I'm very, very thrilled to be the head football coach at Penn State. I'm really looking forward to watching the development of this team going forward."

Tuesday, January 8, 2013

The 2012 team finished 27th in the final AP poll released following Alabama's 44–14 win over Notre Dame for the BCS national championship the night before. The Lions received 90 votes, 29 behind No. 25 Nebraska and five behind Baylor. Other Big Ten teams in the AP poll were: Ohio State (No. 3), Northwestern (No. 17), Michigan (No. 24), and Wisconsin (No. 35).

Thursday, January 17, 2013

O'Brien won the Bear Bryant Coach of the Year Award.

"This is a huge honor for the Penn State program, for a great group of players and a great coaching staff," he said at the ceremonies in Houston. "The other coaches here are phenomenal coaches who have done this for a long time. I've only done this for a year. It shows what type of coaching staff and the type of players we had this year. It means so much to the kids and everyone else who stuck with us. This was a program award. But we've got a long way to go to get Penn State back to what it once was."

Friday, March 1, 2013

The 2012 team captains—Mauti, Zordich, McGloin, Hill, and Yanich—accepted the Thomas Brookshier Spirit Award from the Maxwell Club at the organization's 76th annual gala in Atlantic City. Eight other seniors were sitting at tables in the front row, their head coach onstage because he was the recipient of the club's Coach of the Year Award. Eric Shrive, a junior offensive lineman, also was sitting with the seniors, because he was being honored for his work with Penn State's Uplifting Athletes chapter and its Lift for Life event during a time that the chapter had raised more than $70,000 for kidney research and patients.

Dozens of Penn State football fans were in the sellout crowd today, and they seemed to dominate the applause and cheering throughout the evening. The captains were given a standing ovation when they walked onto the dais to accept the award. Mauti had been selected to speak for the seniors, and he started by asking all the seniors to stand, and they received another standing ovation.

Mauti thanked the Maxwell Club for the award, saying it is meaningful to all the players on the team: "We were not only playing for each other. We weren't playing for a trophy. We couldn't go to a championship game, but awards like this mean more to us than any type of championship trophy, it really does." He said it is an honor to speak for his senior teammates and any one of them could be speaking in his place: "These guys made that commitment under unprecedented circumstances. We chose to play for each other, play for a university, play to help heal a community, to play for things that are bigger than a game of football.... I would be remiss if I didn't recognize our underclassmen, because without them we wouldn't have a team. We had to recruit them to stay with us."

With his fellow cocaptains standing behind him (left to right: Michael Zordich, Michael Yanich, Matt McGloin, and Jordan Hill), Michael Mauti, the inspirational leader of the 2012 team, accepts the Maxwell Club's Thomas Brookshire Spirit Award on behalf of the 2012 team for its "commitment, leadership and outstanding effort" during the season. Photo courtesy of Joe Hermitt, *(Harrisburg) Patriot-News*

Mauti went on to thank O'Brien and all the other coaches, some of whom were in the audience. "Your commitment was equally important," he said, "and everybody was part of that. It was a team thing. To the fans, your support was bar none, every single game, didn't matter where it was, we had Penn State people out there screaming for us, screaming their heads off, like they normally do every week. It was so special. I'll never forget that. [He tapped his heart as the audience clapped and cheered.] Every senior here tonight has graduated or will receive their degree by May of this year. [More cheers and clapping.] Our Penn State alumni, our former football lettermen, those are the guys that really showed us the way, really. I mean, if any of those classes were in our position, they would have done the same thing. They were the guys who really taught us the lesson of integrity, of loyalty and commitment. So we want to thank them for everything they have done and their support as well. [More cheers and clapping.] In closing, I hope you guys have a great evening. It has been truly an honor up here representing these guys, 31 guys that I not only consider my best friends, my teammates, these are my brothers right here. Thank you so much, again."

The audience stood again and clapped, and Mauti and the captains walked off the stage to several chants of "We Are…Penn State!" This was the perfect ending for the remarkable journey of the 2012 football team. Yes, "We Are…Penn State!"

Acknowledgments

I want to thank everyone at Triumph who had a part in making this book possible: Tom Bast, the Triumph editorial director; managing editor Adam Motin; designer Patricia Frey; and especially my manuscript editor, Laine Morreau, for his advice and fine editing.

A special thanks also to Coach Bill O'Brien for writing the foreword and to two members of his football staff who were extremely helpful in my fact-checking: Spider Caldwell and Kirk Diehl.

I also want to thank the following people in the Penn State athletics department who helped me in various ways: Dave Joyner, Fran Ganter, Christine Lauer, Greg Myford, Jeff Nelson, Bud Jim Nachtman, Tony Mancuso, Tommy DiVito, Bob White, Valerie Cingle, and especially Mark Selders.

And a thank-you to those who provided other photographs and video links in the book: Mark Brennan, John Beale, Joe Hermitt, Audrey Snyder (*(Harrisburg) Patriot-News*), and Steve Manuel.

I also want to thank several of the beat reporters from the 2012 season: Genaro Armas, Nate Bauer, Frank Biondi, John Black, Mark Brennan, Scott Brown, Guy Cipriano, Phil Cmor, Donnie Collins, Mark Dent, Bob Flounders, Corey Giger, Matt Herb, Travis Johnson, Ben Jones, Dave Jones, Gordon Jones, Phil

Grosz, Joe Juliano, Derek Levarse, Nate Mink, Walt Moody, Ron Musselman, Tim Owen, Greg Pickel, Mike Poorman, Jeff Rice, Neil Rudel, Rich Scarcella, and Mark Wogenrich.

Among others who helped me were: Dick Anderson, Mark Battiglia, Tom Bradley, Fran Fisher, Laurie Jones, Steve Jones, Jack Ham, Jeff Lowe, John Nichols, Michael Mauti, Rich Mauti, Matt McGloin, Chip Minemyer, Dan Radakovich, Pete Rohrer, Joe Roika, Jon Saraceno, Budd Thalman, and Cindy Zordich.

I also need to acknowledge all the family and friends who were part of the game-day experience for my wife, Carole, and me during the last part of the 2011 season and in 2012: Family—Lori, Mike, Mickey, Carolyn, and Patrick Keating; Scott Prato; Ashleigh and Nate Fennell; Larry and Ruth Harpster; Jim and Barbara Cooper; Bill III and Linda Lundstrom; and Sara Songer. Friends—Don and Barbara Barney; Katie, Don, and Carolyn Bartoo; Richie Barnebie; Jo Ann and Ken Botts; Dave and Rick Browell; Alan Brown and Jerry Olson; Kelly Burns and Chris Howell; Anthony, Anthony Jr., and Francine Campagnini; Joe Cheddar; Mike Corcoran; Joe Davidson; Ron, Judy, Jay, and Randy Falk; Michaelene Franzetta; Billy Gilchrist; Chris and Cathy Goedtel; Joe Kalista; Kathy Kasperik; Brian Kass; Sue Lesko; Ira Miller; Ron Moehler; Paul and Mary Ann Tsompanas; Jason and Larry Rupp; Don Sanders; Eric and Becky Schmidt; Loren and Patti Tobia; Carolyn and Terry Todd; Bob and Elinor Weirman; and Bob Werba.

Finally, without the encouragement, support, indulgence, and proofreading help of my wife, Carole, I could not have written this book. To paraphrase a traditional Penn State cheer and Bill O'Brien's catchphrase from the 2012 season, We Are...One Team!

Appendix I

Penn State's 2012 Senior Class

(As compiled by Mike Poorman, football columnist, StateCollege.com)

Mark Arcidiacono (Holland, PA), No. 73, G—Big presence (6'4", 293 lbs.) on the Nittany Lion practice field.

Joe Baker (West Chester, PA), No. 32, Punter—Backup punter and Philadelphia-area native whose roots are in rugby.

P.J. Byers (Harrison City, PA), No. 45, FB—Active-duty member of the U.S. Navy's officer program, a mature and steady force in the locker room and on the scout team.

Cody Castor (Uniontown, PA), No. 96, DT—Little-used defensive lineman who made a tackle in victory over Purdue.

Derek Day (Harrisburg, PA), No. 24, RB—Hampered by a shoulder injury after starting at Virginia but ran for 109 yards on 33 carries and made nine tackles on special teams.

Andre Dupree (Waldorf, MD), No. 30, FB—Walk-on who carried once in 2011, for five yards against Eastern Michigan.

Emery Etter (Chambersburg, PA), No. 57, KS—Veteran long snapper saw a lot of game action in 2011 but less in 2012 after missing spring drills and having off-season surgery for injury.

Jacob Fagnano (Williamsport, PA), No. 27, S—Versatile special teams and key secondary backup safety, with a career start vs. Indiana and a career-high nine tackles against Ohio.

Mike Farrell (Pittsburgh, PA), No. 78, OT—Cerebral and versatile, moving between left and right tackle, started every game in 2012; three-time Academic All–Big Ten and had 3.40 GPA.

Frank Figueroa (Alexandria, VA), No. 62, OL—Both a guard and a center, often on the cusp of significant playing time.

Patrick Flanagan (State College, PA), No. 15, CB—Diminutive and gutsy native of Happy Valley; uncle (Patrick Chambers) is coach of the Penn State basketball team.

Michael Fuhrman (Pittsburgh, PA), No. 44, KS—Long snapper who waited five years to play but made it pay off with key fumble recovery at Illinois; his father, Chet, was a longtime PSU strength coach.

Jordan Hill (Steelton, PA), No. 47, DT—Second-team All-American and a leader in word and deed with 28 career starts; an active and imposing presence, witness his performance against Wisconsin with career-high 12 tackles with three for losses and two sacks.

Gerald Hodges (Paulsboro, NJ), No. 6, LB—Butkus Award semifinalist who played at a speed and with an abandon that made him No. 4 in the Big Ten in tackles with 109 (45 solo and 64 assists).

Brian Irvin (Orrtanna, PA), No. 82, TE—Former defensive lineman who played in all 12 games in 2011 and performed well in the 2012 Blue-White Game.

Christian Kuntz (Camp Hill, PA), No. 17, WR—Saw some game action in 2012 after grabbing one pass for 17 yards in 2011 and scoring a touchdown in the Blue-White Game.

Evan Lewis (Gettysburg, PA), No. 37, WR/PR—Versatile former QB who was a place-kicker, receiver, and a punt returner, with 11 for 48 yards in 2012.

Pete Massaro (Newtown Square, PA), No. 59, DE—Oft-injured yet owned 15 career starts; a two-time Academic All-American with a 3.85 GPA.

Michael Mauti (Mandeville, LA), No. 42, LB—Unmatched team leader in Penn State football history and the Lions' 97th first-team All-American in history; huge force on the playing field and No. 6 tackler in Big Ten with 96 (49 solo and 47 assists) with three interceptions, including a record-setting 99-yard return at Illinois.

Matt McGloin (Scranton, PA), No. 11, QB—College football's Walk-On of the Year with passing numbers for season and career that are unparalleled in Penn State history; led Big Ten in passing with 279 yards average per game; the picture of perseverance, work ethic, and on-the-field leadership.

Shane McGregor (Ebensburg, PA), No. 2, QB—Career backup known for his classroom prowess, long blond hair, and consistent practice leadership.

Stephon Morris (Greenbelt, MD), No. 12, CB—His 25 career starts were fourth on the team, with the 2012 games played at an elevated level; an articulate and emotional leader of the secondary (fifth on the team in tackles) and defense.

J.R. Refice (Jessup, PA), No. 41, FB—Big, strong, and steady player often mentioned for his contributions on the scout team.

Matt Stankiewitch (Orwigsburg, PA), No. 54, C—Finalist for the Rimington Award, and rightfully so; called blocking signals with experience that came with starts in all of 2011–12 and a 3.42 GPA.

Sean Stanley (Rockville, MD), No. 90, DE—Struggled with a back injury but made 10 starts in 2012, with 35 tackles, including nine tackles for a loss and four sacks.

James Terry (New Castle, DE), No. 93, DT—Big-sized (316 pounds) veteran backup, with a pair of career starts for a very competitive defensive line.

Jamie Van Fleet (Williamsport, PA), LB—Three-year letter-winner who excelled on special teams and played in all 39 possible games before tearing his ACL in December of 2011.

Garrett Venuto (Ithaca, NY), No. 14, QB—Quarterbacks came and went, but Venuto was always there on the scout team and at practice.

Mike Wallace (Silver Spring, MD), CB—Veteran backup known as Mike Walz on campus for his hip-hop stylings that included opening for Big Sean at Hoops Madness, but missed his senior season due to a torn pectoral muscle.

Mike Yancich (Washington, PA), No. 33, LB—Longtime linebacker and honored as the team's outstanding special teams senior player; scored touchdown off of blocked punt against Ohio State.

Michael Zordich (Youngstown, OH), No. 9, FB—An under-appreciated running back and behind-the-scenes team leader until this season when he paired with Mauti to help save the season off the field after NCAA sanctions and backed it up with 301 yards on 80 carries, 15 receptions for 152 yards, and a total of seven touchdowns.

Appendix II

Links to Internet Videos

O'Brien clashes with Tom Brady at New England, December 11, 2011.
http://www.youtube.com/watch?v=33V0hSri6BM

Early morning outside conditioning workout, February 17, 2012.
Mark Brennan, Fight On State: http://www.youtube.com/
watch?v=qgBMHpH4dfM&NR=1&feature=endscreen
Tony Mancuso, Penn State Athletics Communications:
http://www.youtube.com/watch?feature=player_embedded&v=4lsoNy5Am_M

O'Brien and players host pediatric cancer patients from dance marathon,
February 18, 2012.
Mark Brennan, Fight On State:
http://pennstate.scout.com/a.z?s=157&p=10&c=1159816&refid=4781

Rise & Rally, July 31, 2012. http://www.youtube.com/watch?v=OlwZw3titY8

Players present game ball to O'Brien after Navy game.
Tony Mancuso, Penn State Athletics Communications: http://www.gopsusports.com/
blog/2012/09/
exclusive-video-coach-obrien-postgame-locker-room-speech.html

O'Brien and players visit Nittanyville before Northwestern game, October 5, 2012.
Tony Mancuso, Penn State Athletics Communications:
http://www.youtube.com/watch?v=YmtGLaH6moA
http://www.gopsusports.com/blog/2012/10
/video-coach-obrien-seniors-visit-nittanyville.html

O'Brien and payers visit Nittanyville before Ohio State game, October 25, 2012.
Mark Brennan, Fight On State:
http://www.youtube.com/watch?v=i0xwR-UPq6c

Seniors' final practice, November 22, 2012.
Tony Mancuso, Penn State Athletics Communications:
http://www.youtube.com/watch?v=snMkdXTJ5UA&feature=youtube

Senior Day, November 24, 2012.
Tony Mancuso, Penn State Athletics Communications:
http://www.youtube.com/watch?NR=1&v=DhrJPWWXaUk&feature=endscreen
http://www.youtube.com/watch?v=B48-LSgCMu8&NR=1&feature=endscreen

2012 Team wins Brookshier Award at Maxwell Club Dinner, March 1, 2013.
Audrey Snyder, *(Harrisburg) Patriot-News*:
http://videos.pennlive.com/patriot-news/2013/03/video_penn_states_michael_maut.html
Tony Mancuso, Penn State Athletics Communications:
http://www.youtube.com/watch?v=wctUPDXpftc